Spirit of th
Exploring a Unique Irish Landscape
Through The Five Elements

In Irish, 'Boireann' means a stony place, a craggy place and in this wise, insightful and exhilarating book, the stones of the ancient Burren become alive!

Gabriel Rosenstock gabriel-rosenstock.com

A unique spiritual study of the Burren landscape in West Ireland from the perspective of the Five Elements

Spirit of the Burren

Spirit of the Burren: Exploring a Unique Irish Landscape
through the Five Elements

First edition August 2013
Copyright © 2013 by Jackie Queally

For additional information on tours or dowsing workshops e-mail the author at **jackiequeally@gmail.com**

Cover photo Cara Gardner
Cover design Ruth Queally

Published by the author
Printed by Lightning Source
ISBN-10: 0-9541435-9-0
ISBN-13: 978-0-9541435-9-6

Also by this author:

The Lothians Unveiled
Tree Murmurs
The Culdees
Rosslyn and Hinterland
The Spiritual Meaning of Rosslyn's Carvings
The Spiritual Purpose to Rosslyn
Arks within Grail Lands
Eternal Elements

Dedicated to my father,
a quiet man from the gentle hills of West Clare,
who shared a love of curlews, corncrakes and
the Burren of his childhood.

Dedicated to the beloved ancestors

Also dedicated to all the dreamers, healers, seekers and lovers of place.

With special heart-felt thanks to the following:

Invisible guiding angelic hands that made light of the talk and dispelled my intermittent apprehension.

My generous and most kind daughter Ruth Queally for design assistance, layout expertise and talent; PJ Brady for original proof readings; Anthony Clancy for persistent moral encouragement, early proof-reading and friendship; Eileen Connor for her editorial focus and generous comments and local encouragement; Beth Bethany for her wonderful advisory sessions on my book marketing; my long-standing friend Alan Archer Jones for thorough proofing and editorial; Cara Gardner for her wonderful "accidental" photo that adorns the front cover and for spiritual support and friendship; Neil Casey and Tricia Kirby for their ongoing gentle encouragement over recent years and for Tricia's final proofing of the book; Desi Kenny for his expertise; Anthony Peart for gifting me his Burren earth grid; last but not least William Buehler for his depth of knowledge and consistency.

Spirit of the Burren

Contents

Prologue

What is the Spirit of the Burren?
Perhaps it is best defined by what it is not rather than what it is.
It is not a ghost.
It is not a new brand of Irish whiskey.
It is not a legend per se. In fact, it's not a tangible entity at all.

foreigners

It is more like a spiritual presence sensed wherever you go. The Burren is a unique landscape where eerie and vast areas of oolitic limestone dominate the landscape in the west of Ireland. It covers 36.000 hectares of north Clare and south Galway in the Midwest of Ireland, and rises from sea level at the Atlantic to over 300 meters. The area is dominated by treeless, oft-terraced hills shaped to resemble melting jelly from upturned jelly moulds! The weird shapes are a result of many processes whereby the warm shallow sea bed of over 340 million years ago rose to expose fossil-rich layers of limestone, and form classical features of "karst" landscapes in geological terms. Caves, hollows, bare pavements in which a fantastic array of flora thrive in the deep gaps formed, and other more unusual features have attracted world-wide attention from nature specialists. It now has acquired international geopark status. Impressive as such a title is, it does not do the area full justice, in my opinion, as there is a definite yet subtle presence to the place which transcends mere geology. The harder you try to define this presence the more it slips from the fingers of your mind.

Its very elusiveness is what makes it so attractive to so many who seek the quiet, natural places in this busy world. It is also what makes writing this book so difficult a task for me. How can I write about the intangible? How do all the places I visit in the Burren remain in the watery fringes of my memory? Why has the notion of writing a book on the Burren lingered for decades, ever-pecking at my soul?

Perhaps I can compare my reticence to that which I experienced when I ignored a nagging compulsion to write a spiritual guide to Rosslyn Chapel in Scotland. I delayed the project for years. I felt inadequate for the task as that world-famous site was so densely packed with symbolism in its carvings and layout that no one had dared to provide any comprehensive level of interpretation to their meaning. I had been leading private tours there since

1999. It was after the chapel became the last clue in the Da Vinci Code novel that tourism numbers rocketed. Living in the village at the time, I saw how many people seeking deeper truths on their visits perhaps inevitably were offered a fairly superficial rendering of this sacred temple. My unofficial guide to the chapel is thankfully still on sale there to this day. My spiritual interpretations therein are based on a body of knowledge I discovered in 1998 called the Reshel. This knowledge features to a lesser extent in this book. Such knowledge seems to have been operative in temples in Ancient Egypt and filtered through mystery schools to the present day where it became less secretive. Part of the knowledge is encoded in sacred buildings from prehistory onwards. I had always wanted to know the spiritual functions of sacred geometry and I discovered that Rosslyn Chapel embodied the specific Reshel patterns perfectly.

To present the Burren in any meaningful schematic takes insight and discipline to the same degree, much in the same way I took up the challenge of writing my guides to Rosslyn Chapel. Whilst I had a mentor of high intelligence to help me decipher the inner meaning of the carvings there, here in my ancestral homeland I had no such aid. My guides were my experiences, intuition and knowledge. I knew I did not want to present yet another tourist guide to the Burren. Its landscape is designed for a more measured, deeper approach.

Whilst Rosslyn Chapel became a stop-over for many coach tours, the Burren has its equivalent in the Cliffs of Moher, a major tourist attraction that filters most visitors away from exploring the lesser known sites. In fact, most of the Burren yields little traces of a post-industrial era. A vast area with few focal monuments natural or man-made, it has many aspects to it and many hidden places of wonder. Like Rosslyn Chapel, the Burren is a magnet for discerning tourists who come from a wide variety of backgrounds. Many in their own way are seeking the Unknown. The Burren has a mystical quality to it that few deny. Like the chapel too it cannot be read in one visit. Throughout this book I refer to the aforementioned rare Reshel body of spiritual knowledge, in addition to scientific studies that measure the subtle vibrations of physical matter such as rock. I believe that both metaphysical and cutting-edge physical knowledge can complement one another. In the end everything we know and perceive boils down to vibrations. The book is perhaps difficult to categorize as the genre does not fit existing conventional categories. I aim to present a balance of right-brain and left-brain material.

In seeking a structure for this book, the answer was elementary! The chapters would be themed according to the Five Elements.

I had been studying a vibratory healing system that referenced the Chinese meridians, in particular taking into account the Five Element theory of Oriental philosophy. The five inter-dependant elements are Fire, Earth, Metal, Water and Wood. Each chapter opens with an introduction to the particular element in question and ends with a summary to facilitate ease of comprehension.

From studies in esoteric numerology I was aware that the number five can represent a powerful seed thought associated with the process of creation, often identified as female in quality. For instance there were five Celtic seasons that the Ogham tree calendar rotated round. Each season was named after one of the five main vowels spoken in Gaelic, and I had drawn a five-pointed star to illustrate this in my earlier book "Tree Murmurs". The Knights Templar (and later the Freemasons) had adopted the five-pointed star as a representation of divine feminine creative energy. By comparison, the five arms of the star equate with the five elements of the Shen cycle in the Oriental energy system. This cycle illustrates the inter-connectivity of the elements within the whole of life. In this book I highlight the flow of the different elements as a means of describing the Spirit of Burren. The five elements are illustrated overleaf.

In their traditional cycle, the Chinese start with the element of Wood which is concerned with new beginnings and growth. It also is associated with the pioneering spirit, as epitomized by the early Celtic saints. Since Ireland's fundamental element seems to be water, I chose to start the cycle in this book with water. No one can escape water in Ireland, whether in the form of rain, or in the abundance of her lakes and rivers and sea.

In the Burren, the scarcity of surface water might lead an innocent observer to believe that this is a barren region, but this is not so. There are pockets of great fertility among the rocky hills and fields. The oolitic limestone that covers a lot of the Burren retains heat well, and so helps create a micro-climate that is slightly warmer than elsewhere in Ireland. Cattle can remain outside all year round, which helps to enrich the soil. There is a great variety of species of flora. The ecology of the Burren is fragile, and yet remains in a healthy state, in part due to the welcome expert intervention of the Burren Life farming project that works with farmers to ensure support for the local eco system.

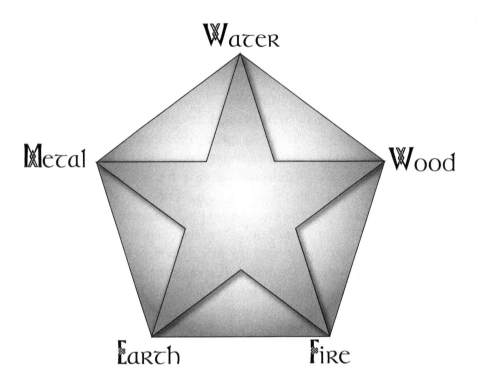

The Burren is a complex area that offers much peace and inner renewal. I found that by exploring its dynamics I have gained precious local knowledge and experience that have formed a template for interpreting spiritual energies in the land. By tracing the serenity in the land you automatically reconnect to your own essence too. I hope that the ideas expressed in this book will inspire others to approach local landscapes that offer a harmony of consciousness. I believe my ideas can be transferred to other areas. I have seen within local farming practice how one inspiring project, Burren Life, influenced not just the locale but also faraway regions. In times when there are widespread feelings of disconnection, areas such as the Burren can infuse visitors with a feeling of reconnection. The serenity and silence of nature reminds many how we are not separate from one another or from nature. If the ideas in this book help reunite people with nature and encourage them to engage with their own area more sensitively and deeply, then that subtle change in   consciousness can weave a positive effect on every avenue of life. The modern world may separate us temporarily, but studies such as provided in this book can help us once again unite.

The longer I stay in the Burren, the less I feel I know. It is rather like asking someone to talk about the Divine. The longer one lives and practises any form of mysticism, the less words become important and the more the silence speaks.

In writing this book I hope to illustrate many salient facts concerning spiritual energies that can perhaps be applied to the study of other sacred landscapes too. This unique fashion of combining spiritual with scientific material has been a challenge to present meaningfully.

This is a task I perform with a trust in the unknown, hoping that the reader not only enjoys reading this but is inspired and intrigued to know more themselves. As with my earlier books, I write this in honour of the sacred essence present in all.

.Jackie Queally August 2013

Element 1: Spirit of Water

WATER DOVE
Your flight
Wings contra-flow
Airily skimming,
Bringer of Peace
Quixotic offering
To a vast cauldron
Erupting from Earth's bowels

Element One

Chapter 1 Water

Water (mostly underground) and holy wells are abundant in the Burren. Consider: all life depends on water. When water is pure and life-giving it is precious, as most water in the world is unfit for human consumption in its natural state, or it may offer little lasting sustenance when it is tapped from recycled sewerage. Holy water or water that is mineral-rich is the best type of water to drink for health of mind and body. Our bodies consist of about seventy percent water and so we have an innate aptitude to resonate with the qualities held in external bodies of water. I will look at the properties of holy water, and the effect that underground and ground water has on the land from an energetic viewpoint later on.

Water permeates all life, and functions as a carrier of mental processes, including the memories of the land it passes through. Water constantly recycles its essence so the pattern can change. In the context of the Burren the water element is strongly connected with the underground system of rivers that abound. There is a geometric earth grid present in the Burren that a skilled geometer presented to me some years ago. This earth grid is a complex geometric pattern that can be drawn over a map of the Burren. The lines represent ley lines, or lines of earth energy, which can be detected using dowsing/divining rods or pendulums. Throughout this book I refer to dowsing from time to time because I find it a useful adjunct to understanding energies.I would like to look a little closer at the dowsing process at this point. I personally came across dowsing when I participated in a spiritual healing course led by a doctor in Yorkshire. Like so many I have taught subsequently, I was surprised to discover I had a knack for finding hidden objects. It confirmed for me a gift of intuition that I had neglected. I found I could enjoy flexing the muscles of intuition by dowsing more often. After several years of dowsing, my view is that it enables you to use your higher mind to find solutions to problems you encounter. The rod or pendulum responds to your inner knowing, and often the answer comes easier when using such external objects as the focal point for the answer. For me it takes me into a space of "still knowing" I possess beneath my cluttered mind.

Ireland as a whole is predominantly shaped by water, which serves as the weaver of the dreamtime. The Spirit of Water boosts the subtle energies of the earth, and in the Burren the underground nature of its rivers serves to boost an earth grid, as well as amplify whatever is present in the realms of human consciousness.

Given the unique qualities that water bears in the Burren, I would like to introduce the Burren from the perspective of water, and examine its effects on the earth/geomantic energies of the Burren. As mentioned in the introduction above, water as an element can be equated with our subconscious meanderings. Here in the Burren where underground rivers invisibly influence the landscape, the power of the subconscious is particularly vivid. It is characterized in a vibrant arts scene including a strong traditional music scene

Water is everywhere. Our bodies are roughly between sixty and seventy percent water, and the planet we live on is made up of 72% water. Ireland is an island largely populated by lakes and rivers and water-clogged lands. The Burren, an area in south Galway and north Clare, is distinguished by its unusual water features: there are numerous underground flows of water that connect with over ground lakes that are forever shifting their shapes. These lakes are called turloughs and are fed by underground springs, their "swallow holes" acting like hidden valves that allow the water a passage in or out of the lake according to the rainfall patterns. The porous limestone of the Burren enables the rain and rivers to percolate down to deeper levels beneath the land. All the rivers are still there, but they rarely reach the surface. It is a speleologist's paradise! The massive labyrinth of caves has to be respected because it can be treacherous to enter.

Like the water, the spirit of the Burren is unseen, but we know it is there. When I use the term "Spirit of the Burren" I am hoping to convey a qualitative or energetic dimension. Such a dimension is not normally measurable within the parameters of everyday scientific thinking. However there have been efforts within the scientific community at large to reach into the less visible worlds and measure frequencies that have a bearing on people's perceptions. I would like to mention these experiments from time to time as it might help to build a picture of how the land interacts with our consciousness. For instance, Burke and Halherg tell us that limestone consists of carbonaceous strata; its electromagnetic properties naturally increase when water moves through it, causing negative electrical charges in the ground (1).(If there is a presence of any trace metal in the rock then the negative charge will increase even more.) The negative ions then accumulate in the ground and boost plant growth and yield. This could well be a contributory factor to plants thriving in the vast limestone areas of the Burren, which may in turn contribute to the known increased yields in goat and cow milk, despite the small pasture lands in the Burren. Moreover, people who have a natural ability to heal others are able to store and release negative healing ions. Such people resonate well with the Burren landscape, since they can sense and respond to the presence of abundant negative ions.

There is a secondary cycle in the Five Element theory that I want to refer briefly to here. That is the Ko Cycle or Way of the Star. In this universal inhibitory cycle water quells the element of fire (as represented by subtle earth energies contained by dragon lines that lay deep within the earth). In other words earth energies that are not conducive to harmony are tamed by the water element. I would imagine that the presence of such voluminous and widespread water streams deep below the land must surely enhance the harmony of the Burren landscape. Much of the underground water in the Burren is fast flowing. I have been fortunate enough to have entered a cave and witnessed a beautiful waterfall and fast-flowing stream. One of the characteristics of fast flowing water is that it can generate an electrical charge, particularly in the area between two separating streams of water. This results in areas on the ground feeling both harmonious and charged. I find the theory of the five elements really holds sway here as I and many others can sense a stillness and a power in the Burren, thanks to the oft-times hidden proliferation of water.

Bees and butterflies live in healthy numbers in the Burren. These creatures are very evocative and also symbolize higher consciousness. Could it be that they are attracted to the region by factors other than the proliferation of pollen from the exquisite Burren flora? Others' research into sound and light wavelengths indicate that animals, birds and insects are highly sensitive to subtle energetic changes in the high frequency range that we as humans are not aware of. We know now that our brains are capable of receiving information in these areas that we are not able to cognitively process. According to the current societal paradigm, our experiences of other dimensions that are less visible are real only once science proves them to exist; and yet in less "civilised" societies seers and mystics were long recognized as having this ability to penetrate other realms of reality. In the twenty first century, the gap between the Seen and Unseen is thankfully narrowing a little as science progresses more. There seem to be many subtle laws governing reality. Many states of being described in metaphysical experiences echo the descriptions of what occurs at sub-atomic levels of matter. I believe that perceptions of reality alter, according to the perceiver and that when this is understood there is room for accepting other levels of reality which people can experience. It paves the way for greater understanding of one another.

This book, Spirit of the Burren, is addressing a multi-layered reality, far removed from the confines of that which a media-driven culture seeks to impose. It is a skill or a gift to be able to perceive the layering of realities, and to discern those levels that are higher in frequencies and so closer to the Divine energies that I believe support and create everything in nature. In this book I present the case that the Burren contains very high energies that make it a holy place. Holy wells are an essential underlying influence on the landscape. The proliferation of holy wells in the Burren is testament to its enduring quality of sacredness. They are an integral feature of the Burren visually and culturally still. Energetically speaking, wells are an essential underlying influence on its landscape.

When I moved closer to where my ancestors came from on the edge of the Burren in late 2008 my drinking water came from a local spring. Thankfully I have had access to natural spring water ever since. Early memories show us what has shaped us. I have always appreciated natural water. I grew up in London where I learnt the tap water came from recycled sewerage. In contrast, my grandfather was a water diviner living on the Atlantic seaboard of the Burren. He would set off with his hazel rod to find water on some remote farm. One of my first memories is of fetching water from the well two fields away, with a donkey to help carry the water back to the small farmhouse. My grandmother always let others draw water from the well – neighbours, travellers and campers. She was a very gracious woman of quiet dignity, whom people loved to call on and listen to her tales of the Sidhe (fairy folk) and other stories. She respected herself and other people, and others in turn respected her. I got a deep sense that she was bound to the land, and her stories were like spells that bound all who were listening to the land forever more. Whenever people entered or left her home she would bless them with a sprinkle of holy water and a quiet murmuring prayer. It was as if she gave them a little piece of her heart in this momentary act. The little act made a deep impression on me as a child. Much as I loved the liveliness of London where I grew up, here was a world apart, full of grace and timelessness. No one hurried in those days in Ireland!

It has been scientifically asserted that water stores memory of human thoughts and emotions. Dr Masaru Emoto in Japan has claimed for years that water responds to our thought forms (see Further Reading Section at end of book). Water is a beautiful vehicle to carry our prayers, and often wells have held a special place in the hearts of Irish people. They also refused to take in any branch of a tree that grew on the site of a holy well. People went to pray at these holy wells. I personally heard a story recently of an old man who had been both blind and deaf when young. One night he went to an ancient well, which was off the beaten track. Knowing of its great healing properties, he lay beside it all night. He returned in the morning cured of both blindness and deafness. The well commands awe and respect even in someone who was not an overtly religious person and he duly prayed there all night. The miraculous cure was the answer to his prayers in his opinion. He did not make a fuss of the miracle but continued his daily life unobtrusively.

There is a great belief in the efficacy of prayers and in the curative properties of the wells among the old folk where I live. Often we can receive answers to our problems when resting by their clear waters. Again referring to my childhood visits to Ireland, when accompanying my relatives on their visits to holy wells, I noticed how much emotion the women would inject into their prayers. I know from studying prayer (both as a liberal theology student and from reading books by Greg Braden and others much later) that a prayer is a dead prayer without engaging the feelings (see Further Reading Section at end of book). When spoken from the heart a prayer can truly fly. I remember my childhood visits to the holy wells with those Catholic women. I sensed their prayers were mechanical, but their feelings left a deep impression on me. It is best when engaging with emotions in a prayer to have a clear intent or focussed thought. If not, the emotions can dissipate into the ether and the prayer is not "activated". Neville Goddard, who in the early part of the twentieth century inspired many in America to practise more effective forms of praying, understood how important it was for a prayer to be spoken with positivity and heart-felt gratitude (see Further Reading Section at end of book). Modern writers such as Greg Braden, who write on positive thinking as a form of prayer, owe much to this long-forgotten Barbadian citizen of the USA. Neville spoke ahead of his time, and was not recognized for the depth of his message which was deeply Christian and also universal. Water is a perfect medium to facilitate deeper prayer. The very act of baptism, in churches, uses water with intent and positivity when initiating the newborn into the flock. In pre-Christian times water was used similarly. Holy wells are not limited to the Christian period because water has always been a sacred medium.

As a medium, water is highly sensitive to our feelings as well as our thoughts. We can communicate with our innermost selves more easily besides the "holy" waters. Further, a watery environment can inspire us to dream both when awake and while sleeping, as water works with the subconscious, giving it space to reveal its inner workings. One farmer in the Midlands in Ireland has built a series of sacred structures on his land, all laid out with careful thought to the overall design and orientation. The focal point of the complex is a deep well whose water contains numerous precious minerals. There, he has built a dome or cairn over the well that is approached via a passageway, resembling that of a court cairn. Apart from his many years of sheer dedication in constructing the site he has equally done a lot of inner work while sitting beside his well, and listening to the waters! Thus the structures have evolved into a remarkable temple landscape, all based on inspiration that he has received while reflecting at the well. I was struck by his insights and humility, both aspects that he felt were gifted to him, by the spirits of the water he met, when meditating at the well.

Water has always been associated with temples. It is a necessary component in places associated with prayer and meditation because water acts like a memory pool constantly recycling spent emotions. It also acts as a protector, shielding the holy site from negative earth energies and forces. The priests bless the water and this prayer of intent creates a force field around the church for instance. If the water is pure in quality it will also create a vortex that affects the atmosphere for those near the water. I will return to the energetic properties of water throughout as it is a constant feature in understanding the Spirit of Burren.

Water is present beside most sacred sites. Holy water absorbs light at different frequencies as observed when tested using infrared spectroscopy. It is also free from bacteria and contains beneficial natural minerals. Pure water in turn will create a spinning energy vortex according to F. Silva (2). This in turn creates an electrical charge, which generates an electro-magnetic field, with the result that the water in the well is indeed holy and charged.

When we drink holy water it vitalizes our blood that carries information round our body. It also affects our brains which are made of about ninety percent water. We are imbibing the prayers of those who went before us as well as the natural qualities of the water as water holds memory as Emoto proved. Silva also points out (3) that our sensory organs are more receptive to extra-sensory experiences when stimulated by energized water and refreshed blood.   In the Burren wells are invariably situated close to the hermitages of early Christian monks and saints. The well was a constant source of inspiration to those who followed the hermetic tradition. Like our modern-day mystic farmer, they treated water with great respect. When wells are mistreated misfortune can result. It seems particularly unwise to tamper with deep artesian wells.

When I lived in Edinburgh, there existed a sacred artesian well that the monks of Holyrood used in the production of their sacred mead, from the twelfth century onwards. After construction started in June 1999 for Scotland's own new parliament over this same ancient site, the well head was accidentally drilled into (unbeknown to many inhabitants of the city), and copious flows of water were exuberantly flowing into the foundations of the new building. Many of the premises on the neighbouring Royal Mile suffered from flooding too. It took at least six months to stem the flow from this holy well. The parliament's chosen architect Frank Meralles and the First Minister for Scotland Donald Dewar both died around this time in 2000 from a brain haemorrhage and tumour respectively. Both men were in the prime of their lives. It seemed a very unlikely coincidence and I remember at the time wondering if some sort of curse had been placed on the project, particularly as costs eventually rose between ten and forty times the original estimates! Architect and lecturer Professor Brian Adams from Dundee University was a master pupil in Feng Shui. He analysed the site, and publicly declared the design was very negative for its auspicious location within Holyrood Park, a wildlife and recreational area formerly used as an official sanctuary. Moreover there are strong leys (lines of earth energies) traversing the site, and so to build a parliament on such a site requires that the politicians are remarkably clear in their intentions, or the highly charged energies will work against them. Whenever one inhabits or works in an area that has high earth energies or strong leys it is vital to be aware of them and act accordingly, as every event or mental thought is amplified at such places.

Later we will look at the leys of the Burren and see how this can affect consciousness positively. NASA has proven that water attracts geomagnetic lines (4). There is a preponderance of such lines in the Burren. Where underlying water streams coincide with strong electro-magnetic leys above, a place of power will result. This combination is a good siting for gatherings such as a church requires, since the site would be highly charged. The localised energies no doubt can amplify prayers, and in turn these purer thoughts or prayers magnify the energy of the water beneath it. This circle of reciprocal energies can subtly ripple out over a whole area. In the same way, a hermit, living in a local cell, could affect a whole area in a large magnetic ripple effect. Compare this with a parliament whose focus is on intellectual debate rather than peaceful prayer. In either case, water serves to amplify the thought processes that take place at the site. An artesian well, such as exists at Holyrood, has a particularly strong boosting effect on the emotional state of those in the vicinity. It has to be handled wisely, and spiritual rather than political affairs are suited to such sites.

On the eastern fringes of the Burren, the rivers flow both on the surface and underground. I must confess to a total fascination with this region, with its numerous turloughs. The main town in the region is Gort, who over the years earned itself the title "Home to the Stranger", probably stemming from the overriding generosity of its ancient High King Guaire. In the following chapter I will return to this interesting name, in the light of its early Christian roots. Despite a lack of visible rocky outcrops, the Gort Lowlands are part of the Burren region geologically speaking. The sweeping expanse of flat limestone pavements peter out short of Gort and more traditional grasslands take over. However the area was once covered by the same limestone as seen in the Burren hills, slightly to the west. Over millions of years the limestone pavement has disintegrated through rain slowly dissolving it. In the future all of the Burren will revert to a landscape typical of what can be seen around Gort, unless unforeseen drastic shifts in the Earth's crust take place. There is a myth that I think portrays well the divide between the Burren and the area to the east. It highlights the importance of water acting as a boundary, and it takes place in the rolling Slieve Aughty hills to the east of Gort. The tale comes from the Dindschensas written in the twelfth century, compiled from earlier documents. Note that "dind" means "a noteworthy place" and that "schensas" means "stories that are mainly mythological". Often myths are describing stellar movements in the skies, echoed by more subtle influences and energies deep within the earth, that all shape the lay of the land. Here is my version of the tale:

During the time that the people of the goddess Danu (known as the Tuath de Danaan) ruled Ireland there lived a princess with the extraordinary name of "Echtge the Horrible" (her name is an old/ medieval Irish version of the word Eachtaigh/ Aughty). Her father was a kind and gracious king. He was either a warrior named "Strong Dedadd", or else "Nuada of the Silver Arm". He married Boinn, which is also the name of the river near Tara where they ruled. Echtge was reared as was the custom by a foster parent-in her case Moach the Bald, who lived at a place called Echtair. The Fir Bolg kings had been defeated by the De Danaan. Fergus Mac Ruidi was Cup Bearer to Genn and Genann who were Fir Bolg kings. A cup bearer has a most trusted position in society. His own race now in decline, Fergus wanted to marry Echtge, of the highly skilled, somewhat mystical race of De Danaan. Fergus owned vast tracts of land stretching from the Plain of Moenmoy to the sea, and he bestowed a hill range on his beloved Echtge that to this day bears her name in the Slieve Aughty Mountains. As part of her dowry, Echtge gave two milch cows, placing them on either side of the river that bears the Anglicized name "Owendalulagh" or in Irish Abhainn dá Loilgheach ("river of the two milch cows") to this day. The cow on the east side of the Owendalulagh was nearly barren whereas the cow on the west side yielded thrice more milk.

The contrasting nature of the cows reflects the two aspects of the area. The land to the east lies in eastern range of Slieve Aughty hills, where its acid soils are often clad with monoculture pine forest plantations. Yet these dense sandstones and mudstones would have hosted native oak forest there at the time of the legend. The divide took place on the townland of Derrybrien, meaning "oak wood of hospitality/Brian". Derrybrien hosts a tree that is said to yield holy oil. The tree is now in a cemetery. On the summit of Derrybrien there is a highly visible wind energy farm. To the west of the divide lies an attractive fertile plain that stretches towards the Burren hills, upon which in more recent history many English made their demesnes. The limestone of the Burren contains within it particles of quartz that have healing qualities. The Burren is, in my opinion, a distinctly feminine landscape. Its hills do not have any uniformity to them and they fold and rise in the most graceful forms. By contrast the eastern hills appear more broody and masculine in nature. Being of the fairy blood herself, Echtge bestowed fertility on the Burren side of the river, where she owned land all the way to the sea. It was

11

in this land that the legendary Tuatha de Danaan seemed to reign supreme.

Who were these Tuatha de Danaan? Some believe they no longer exist, but I have met those in Ireland who believe that their blood still courses through the veins of those gifted with second sight. They were the second oldest, and arguably oldest, race in Ireland: some say they were a sept of magicians and skilled craftsmen living among the first race the Fir Bolg (meaning the Bag men, referring to their period of slavery when they were forced to carry earth in bags!) The Danaan were said to originally have been Nemedians from Scythia. Legend tells that these ancient Scythians came from the area around Greece, where they had been enslaved by invaders. They reached Ireland in the Bronze Age when they apparently integrated into the Fir Bolg race. Recent DNA evidence supports the idea of the legend. It shows that the majority of Irish blood stems from the eastern Mediterranean around 4000BC (5). The goddess of the De Danaan was known as the Strong One who Dwells in the Silence. Later the De Danaan became semi-mythical and probably confused with the gods that they worshipped. Legend says they were forced to live in caves and underground places when the Iron Age race of Milesians invaded, possibly around 2000BC. Deep within the earth the De Danaan acquired their fairy blood, mixing with the elves and the other supernatural beings. In slightly earlier times than now there was a long held belief that the unoccupied forts were haunted at night by these semi-mythical folk. This ability to remain as spirits, who inhabit the underworld, marks the De Danaan out as a special race apart, long associated with the Burren. They probably sought out the Burren from the early days of their enforced move underground. The wedge tombs and portal tombs (dolmens) dating from 3000-1800BC would have been constructed during their reign. These structures proliferate in the Burren, with many in the east Burren lying submerged in the deeper soils.

Archaeological studies of ancient monuments in County Clare (6) show that the Burren has the oldest monuments, stretching back to 4200 BC (the start of the Neolithic era). Early kitchen middens have been found along the Atlantic shores of the Burren where my ancestors lived. No doubt the local population created monuments for their dead. The thin fertile soils of the Burren supported lighter woodland that was easier to clear than the heavier forests inland on deeper soils.

Interestingly Scythia is the source race of ancient Scotland too, according to Walter Bowers of Inchcolm Abbey who wrote the Scotti Chronicum in the twelfth century. The legend of Princess Scota is mentioned in both Irish and Scottish mythology. She is supposed to have resided on Tara when there were many Pagan temples there.(7). She came from Egypt with a retinue of noble people whose bloodline appears to have been connected to the Tuatha de Danaan. I get a sense that these people were noble families who controlled the wealth of their nations via their ownership and skilled use of metals.

Returning to the marriage of Fergus and Echtge, the couple were consummating a transference of power and its associated consciousness. Fergus symbolizes the older consciousness of the Fir Bolg. Fergus was transferring the power of his own race to the new incoming consciousness by marrying Echtge of the De Danaan. Fergus's role as a cup bearer to his high kings is worthy of more comment, although I realise I am straying off the subject of water! I am doing this for a reason. Fergus would test the wine on behalf of his kings to ensure it was safe to drink so he held the supreme position of trust within the tribe. Passable wine apart, the Cup Bearer as a titular role is highly relevant within the terminology used in the Reshel, based on geometer William Buehler's mystical research into ancient Hebrew as spoken in ancient Egypt. The Cup Bearer carried the karmic responsibility for the whole tribe or race. When ascribing geometrical nodes to ancient Hebrew meanings Buehler has realised that the Cup Bearer is often associated with a key geographical position in the land, which would equate with the control position for an "earth grid". The interpretation of these patterns of sacred geometry lies beyond the remit of this book. I will refer to this meta science in later chapters, and only wish to say here that the legend more than likely carries deeper meaning than is generally understood. By applying the Reshel knowledge to legend it can become a useful method of interpreting deep layers of meaning. Certainly, in the case of Scottish legends I have found this to be so. The Fergus and Echtge legend suggests that the region around Gort bears a strong significance for Ireland's elementals, or devic energies, as linked with the De Danaan tribe in mythology. It is in this same geographical area that Yeats and Lady Gregory dwelt, gathering Irish fairy tales both far and wide.

A river flows from Derrybrien into Lough Cutra, Ireland's largest privately owned lake. The shape of this lake bears an uncanny resemblance to the map of Ireland (the north and south are taken as a whole island in this instance). There are supposed to be seven islands in the lake. Seven is a magical number associated with the divine feminine in mysticism. Cutra is named after Cutra, a De Danaan prince who fled Tara when his father was defeated. Cutra's brother died in battle with Cuchullain and is buried in a cairn in nearby Kilbeacanty, close to Lough Cutra.

The local mythological and geological references hopefully have set the scene better for our main concept here: water. The routes that water take play a distinct part in shaping the quality of any area. In the eastern Burren around Gort water plays the part of the trickster. A wise fool, a creator of worlds, he blurs the line between above and below. This mental attribute is mirrored in the physical world as the river dips above and dives below the earth's surface. Traditionally the trickster is so flexible in mind and spirit he is believed to bear messages from the gods. A trickster is unsettling and transformative. His behaviour often unearths the collective subconscious. The rivers adjust to the bedrock and flow in and out of the landscape in a most unpredictable manner. For instance, the aforementioned Owendulagh river flows out of Lough Cutra, and then as the Beagh river winds its way as far as a complex of collapsed river caves near Gort, where it disappears. Striking features known as the Churn, the Ladle and the Devil's Punchbowl mark the course of the river here as it marks the legendary divide between the Slieve Aughtys and the Burren hills. The whole area is a type of crossing place. Crossing places can feel a little mysterious and other-worldly. I would ascribe a sort of timeless, ill-defined androgynous air to such areas. In the Gort lowlands there is a constant mixing of feminine and masculine energies due in no small part to the action of the river, which constantly changes its name! The river will flow above ground for a short distance only to suddenly disappear and then reappear above ground under a new guise a short distance away. Tracing the river through and beyond Gort is a mystery drama in itself! Where the river exits at Cannahowna (head of the Owen river) there is a massive underground cave headed by a long rock upon which you can stand. Stand here on a moonlit night and dare to defy the presence of some ethereal natural energy! (During a recent divining workshop I led locally I took the group to Cannohowna. Someone took some photographs of us divining at the face of the cave. When developed a series of intensely bright lights showed up in the cave photos.

I also view this crossing place as representing a still point in the landscape, where the energies are not so polarized. This sort of energy can have a disarming effect on its inhabitants as it is not as sharply defined as a distinctly feminine or masculine area. It might make people more susceptible to negative emotions.

Adding to the general confusion of river courses here is the aqua labyrinth of swallow holes that control the swelling and sinking of the lakes (turloughs). In dry periods the fields take over where once the lakes flowed, revealing large openings in the bedrock. These features can be dangerous. In Rasheen Turlough in east Galway according to a local inhabitant a horse and rider were crossing the lake bed when the horse fell down one such swallow hole. The rider escaped but the horse was swept away in an underwater channel and sadly drowned! The east Burren river and cave system is a complex under-mapped region of the earth, with water creating mysterious undercurrents that shift and adapt through the years, with no outward warnings. Once I went to film an area where three underground rivers are said to emerge from deep within the land - when there I created a poem that was quite dark in tone (for me!) (8). The very next week a popular and highly experienced Polish diver went missing in the very same cave I had visited. He too never returned.

The effect that underground water plays on the human psyche should not be under-estimated. Perhaps it makes people generous! In Celtic times the area became associated with the generous king Guaire who welcomed strangers. His cousin Colman was a saint whose ecclesiastical prowess spread throughout the west. At the turn of the twentieth century Lady Augusta Gregory gathered much folklore from this region and championed the re-establishment of native culture.

Perhaps it is not surprising that she lived alongside one of the largest turloughs in the region: Coole Turlough. While logically you might argue that she lived there because her husband Sir Robert had an estate there, the events that transpire are often guided by an invisible hand that I believe is not Destiny alone. When faced with an element of choice, as in the case of those who could afford to build estates (or indeed erect cathedrals), I believe that people gravitate towards one location or another according to the subtle qualities inherent in the land that they can resonate with. I observed that  different river valleys in Cumbria where I used to live would attract different groups of people, with like minds. As a sensitive, I sensed that the human psyche is drawn to an area whose resonance matches that quality they have an affinity with. Once people are living in an area, the earth's resonances can influence them to behave in ways that correspond to its very nature.

Water serves to amplify the energies inherent in the land. It is the main reason many temples of all religions incorporate a body of water in their designs. There are areas in nature too that are sacred, and they nearly always contain a large reservoir of water as a necessary component. Water stores, processes and responds to our mental processes. Rivers transport all human thoughts and events throughout the land. When water lies beneath the ground it will have an exaggerating effect on the subtle electro-magnetic frequencies inherent in the land. Lakes and rivers that disappear underneath us create an amplified field of energy that we might not be aware of since it is not visible. Water as an etheric body is in psychic terms "monopolar" rather in the way I described the area around Gort. I might have initially sensed Gort, in that manner because I was tuning into the element of water below its surface. (I will explore this monopolar nature further laster on in the book.) There is a lot of underground water in the Gort region. Unlike the Burren hills though, there is a relative absence of limestone pavement to cap the water. It is very important that the water can flow freely through an area because blockages can have a negative effect on the thinking processes of its inhabitants. When water disappears so often deep beneath the surface there is a danger that impediments are not detected. Sometimes plastic fertilizer bags blow into the streams where they are carried underground, causing not just physical damage to wildlife and the environment, but also helping to foster psychic blockages. Water is a sacred commodity. Ideally it should be respected by all. It is not just a commodity to consume. It is our very life source.

I like to call the area around Gort the Underbelly of the Burren because it can cause deep stirrings, typically ascribed to the sacral chakra of a human. (Human emotions are linked to energy centres called chakras in the human body. These are often detected and worked on by healers.) In its negative aspect, fear and embarrassment will be stirred with this energy. According to oriental medicine the sacrum is in turn twinned with the throat chakra- and small wonder that this area has attracted poets and writers from the time of the Celtic Revival until the present day.

In the Gort Lowlands, the complex system of rivers and turloughs truly create a unique habitat. There is even a tidal turlough named Caherglassaun Lough (near Garrylands Nature Reserve behind Coole Park) whose marine waters mix with the incoming springs on the coast at Kinvara. In the olden days, fishermen on curraghs used to draw alongside these springs and fetch their drinking water from them in the sea! The notion of a tidal turlough reminds me of the moon that affects the tides. A lunar lake is deeply feminine in nature, emptying and refilling constantly. It is a gateway into the deep under - realm in fairy terms, drawing on the chthonic powers of the deep Earth. It will flow into the fairy presences in the landscape, which according to Coleston Brown (8) are connected with initiation and regeneration. It is interesting that the turlough lies very close to Coole Lough, where characters such as Yeats often walked. Many of those who frequented Coole Park held a deep interest in the mystical side of life. This region around Coole Park is deeply connected to the Irish dream state that is so heavily associated with water. It is an archetypal landscape for the fey or fairy energies. How is this so?

The answer lies in the rivers. Rivers are to the planet what we experience as the nervous system in our bodies. They are like neural pathways connecting consciousness to the planetary life blood. What happens when these nerves temporarily disappear and then reappear again and again, as in the case in the eastern Burren? The rivers will collect subtle energies from deep below the surface and then bring them to the surface to mingle with denser energies. This creates a highly sophisticated energy system. From the point of view of a psychic, this would suggest that subtle energies are being constantly re-stimulated. The simpler the nervous system the denser the life force. Here in the Gort Lowlands, there is a more dilute, almost homeopathic life force that can easily be overlooked in the humdrum of everyday survival. It will play an influence nevertheless, even though people might be unaware of its existence.

To the west, in the more widely known Burren landscape, the rivers rarely surface. When the underlying shale is exposed, as in the Caher Valley, a babbling brook can surface. The interplay between rock and water is important. The Burren is a fairly large land mass of mainly oolitic limestone, underpinned by a relatively unknown or unheeded pattern of water streams. Oolitic limestone is a particular type of limestone, ubiquitous in the Burren but rarely found elsewhere in Ireland. It is formed by each grain of sand surrounding itself with an egg-like granule of calcium carbonate. The sand consists of quartz, which is a healing mineral that vibrates at a high frequency conducive to meditating. So the Burren contains a potent underlying rock type that is conducive to a life of prayer and reflection. It is thus the combination of the water and rock that creates a magical pulse that weaves its way through the land in the Burren. It helps expand one's consciousness in a gentle way, rather as we experience ourselves in a dream state. It is such a good thing that there is no intensive industry utilizing water in the area, as that might taint the underground supply. There are strict controls too on the use of fertilizers on farms in the region. Fertilizer run off is detrimental to the quality of water and it would penetrate levels beneath the surface where water runs.

In many ways, the underground water has its corollary in the space that surrounds our planet. Both are spaces that in themselves are not polarized, but which contain polarities – land mass contains polarities in the case of water and star systems do so in the case of outer space. Within the land, water shapes the land and the land in turn shapes the water through releasing its trace elements into the water. Remember, everything is connected. It is a spiritual truth that the deep energies of the inner earth are reflected in the stellar energies. The Earth mirrors the whole universe, and our planet contains all cosmic matter with which it is connected.

1 Seeds of Knowledge Stone of Plenty 2005 John Burke and Kaj Halberg Council Oak Books ISBN 1-57178-184-6 p 150
2 The Divine Blueprint 2012 Freddy Silva Invisible Temple ISBN 13: 978-0-9852824-4-8 P171
3 Silva ibid p 174
4 Silva ibid p180
5 Patricia Balaresque et all University of Leicester 2013
6 Mapping by Carleton Jones an expert archaeologist in the Burren indicates a high density of Neolithic monuments. See The Burren and the Aran Islands 2006 Carleton Jones ISBN 978-1-903464-49-6
7 The Book of the Taking of Ireland Section 2 - Early History of the Gaedil tr.ed. RS Stewart Macalister 1939
8 Secrets of Fairy landscape Coleston Brown / Jessie Skillen 2012 Green Fire Publishing ISBN 978-0-9865912-2-8

Water

SPIRIT OF WATER

Concluding remarks: There is an abundance of hidden water and holy springs and wells in the Burren. Water carries mental thoughts and responds to mass consciousness. It stores the memory of the land in its rivers and lakes, constantly recycling the energies. In the Burren, the rivers serve to influence humans on a vital yet subtle energetic level, for most of the time the rivers are underground, invisibly boosting the energies of the land.

Consider how all life depends on water. It feeds all plant forms. Trees are so vital to the planet on many levels, beginning with the role they play in attracting rains and storing rainwater in their root systems. Humans are drawn to the forest to clear their thoughts and regenerate themselves psychically. It as if the water we store in our body resonates with the water stored in the trees, enabling us to clear and purify our thoughts.

Element 2: The Spirit of Wood

ETERNAL OFFERINGS
A makeshift cross
Bears tidings of our makeshift times
Yet the tradition of the hidden retreat
Still draws us in.
A magnet of stillness
With altars poised
As if they could sing
In another dimension.
Songs of deep love, hope, forgiveness and above all
Peace.

Element Two

Chapter 2 Early Christians

On a purely physical level wood is present in trees, providing sustenance for life and creating a living landscape that creatures can thrive in. In fact much of life as we know it depends on the continued existence of forests. On an emotional level, the wood element holds the energy of the pioneering spirit, fuelled by forward thinking processes. I associate this aspect of the wood element with the Spirit of Early Christians. I invite the reader to appreciate the past knowledge held in this area when Ireland was at its intellectual superiority within the world of Christendom. The early Christian monks were robust, wise, intelligent and deep-thinking people. It is perhaps what the Burren is most closely associated with in the eyes of the Irish people. Starting with the more familiar human element, I introduce several themes in this second chapter. In subsequent chapters I develop each theme further.

Many early saints lived in the Burren and offshore on the Aran Islands in the wide mouth of Galway Bay. Here I wish to draw particular attention to a pioneering group of Christians known as the Culdees, about whom there is scant written evidence. They were a non-hierarchical group who focussed on a direct knowing of God without the need for an intermediary. Their links went back to ancient Egyptian mystery schools , and they utilized pre-Christian sites on their wide travels. Thus the Culdees married the old Druid ways with the new consciousness of Christianity that followed the teachings of Christ, apparently in ways that the Roman church obliterated in later centuries.

Since early adulthood I have sensed that the Burren played host to these pioneering Christians, who were more mystical by nature than mainstream thinking might portray. Within a wider geographical context, we can start to glean the possibility that this was the case. The element of wood also reminds me of the ancient trees that once graced much of the landscape in Ireland, including the Burren in the areas where the surface rock was not so prevalent. In parts, remnants of old oak and hawthorn groves remain, and are particularly enchanting when growing over "fairy rings" that man has wisely left undisturbed. In the so-called Celtic period (late Iron Age) the Druids worshipped in tree groves, and as Christianity took over, the early proponents of the new religion still revered the powers of nature.

Ancient prayers in Gaelic testify to this. These early Christians tended to worship in the same groves as did their ancestors the Druids. For instance St Colman, who founded Kilmacduagh Monastery in the seventh century, lived in a cave within a deep hazel thicket, below Eagle's Rock in the Burren. I particularly love Lough Avalla Farm within the Burren National Park, where there is a beautiful grove containing a small ancient fort/fairy ring close by a holy well. There, in that well-tended spot, the watercress thrives in its clear springs. It is easy to imagine a hermit living here once. The hermit monks of the Burren were truly pioneers, creating a new way of thinking and living. Their lives had to be led with discipline in order to achieve anything beyond mere survival. It took a certain stubbornness to carve out their new way of living here in the rocky desert – this strong will is part of the Wood Element.

There are several places of natural beauty within the Burren that are associated with local Irish saints. Most of these places are hazel groves that provide the predominant vegetation cover in the Burren. The Culdees could marry and hold small pockets of land according to early travel reports from Italy and Greece. These travel reports reference the UK, particularly Scotland, and in the early centuries there was a shared hermetic tradition between Scotland and Ireland, with local travel between both countries. (1) According to some, my surname means "of the hazel grove", so perhaps I have ancestral links to this saintly group!

To summarise so far, the new thinking associated with the new religion corresponded well with the element of Wood in the oriental energy system. I perceive in the works of the late John O'Donohue (1956-2008) a revival of this art (see Further Reading section). John was an inspiring ex-priest who lived in the Burren all his life and who embraced the important messages that nature yields unendingly. His poetry and prose was much loved by all, and he also revived the tradition of open air prayer and worship within a broader Christian practice. Flexibility of thinking and focussed yet gentle prayer hallmarked John and his ancestral holy ones. Wood is certainly a good starting point in our cycle as it colours the mental processes and actions that follow. At the spiritual level, there is a truth expressed in:

Nothing is created without a pre-form which is thought.

Using the universal law that thought precedes form, Barbados-born Neville Goddard (1905-1972) had heralded a plethora of self-styled gurus, who somewhat mistakenly channelled his positive affirmation process into "get rich quick" formulae. In reality Goddard shed great light on the interplay between the subconscious and normal states of consciousness, showing us how we may tap into an eventually become the supra-consciousness (God spark) that resides in each of us. The key was to awaken the subconscious and lead a more fruitful life purposely created by the imagination that dwells in each of us. The excellent research of contemporary writer Greg Braden (2) on the nature of prayer takes these mental processes back to their roots, where spirituality played a large role still, as advocated by Neville Goddard(3). (Braden tells us that toward the end of his life, Neville spoke more about his Biblical interpretation methods as uncovering the true message of Christ. At this point he lost most of his followers, who seemed more interested in a result-driven psychology than what they may have deemed a mystical path!)

Again, while the wood element is associated on the psychological level with the pioneering spirit and new thinking, it obviously manifests as trees in the physical or natural world. Trees provide vital grounding mechanisms for our thoughts. For instance we often feel cleared of negative thoughts and over-thinking when we walk in the forest. Moreover the spirit of the land is intrinsically tied up with the spirit of the trees. As Andrew St Ledger the dedicated founder of the Woodland League in Ireland puts it:

"The spirit of the land needs to manifest itself through forest, and there is a probable loss of spirit in the Irish psyche that could be restored throuugh conscious reconnecting with the forest, as trees are an integral part of healing for the people."

I like to view the "saints" who chose to dwell in solitude, in forest caves and hermit cells, as living in balance with nature and in a healthy symbiosis. The monks communed with nature in general, in ways that we could emulate. More specifically we overlook trees at our peril. The trees served to ground the monks' prayers, and clear their negative thoughts. They can do the same for us now.

The Culdees settled in quiet corners of the Burren, undisturbed by human affairs. The type of Christianity they practised may not be very recognizable from that which is practised today. I purport that an earlier strain of Christianity, more aligned with nature and less with dogma and doctrinal matters, prevailed in the region. The roots of this tradition go back to Jerusalem in the first century CE, to the period when the Romans were sacking the city of its religious sects. Among the many fleeing sects were the Nazorean and Essenes, whose roots go back to ancient Egypt and the initiatory traditions therein. Some of their ideals resurfaced in other parts of the world beyond the Mediterranean, perhaps borne by the diasporas who fled by sea.

It is difficult to write authoritatively on early Christian history because so many records were lost, destroyed or never created due to a prevailing oral tradition (as in the case of the Culdees). We may consider history a discipline, though it is in my belief more accurate to consider it a study of the shadows generated by past events. Each historian interprets an event according to their powers of discernment as to what was the truth of the event. Depending on the bias of the historian different interpretations inevitably surface. I consider a hearsay approach to times that have little recorded history as uninspiring, without recourse to other faculties than mere folklore or accepted traditions. I value mystical thinking as a source for contemplating historical events, as conventional history concerns itself with surface phenomena that do not yield much qualitative insight. When we can indulge ourselves in a fresh perspective, much might be gained. Mystical thought (such as the writings of Rudolf Steiner) suggests that each nation has a role to play in the divine drama of our planet. In this region of Europe mystical thought maintains that Ireland has always held the key to the sacred knowledge of the nature kingdoms, or elementals. This knowledge belongs to what I would call it the lower heavens, a term which embraces far more than the watered down perceptions we have inherited from our predominantly commercial age. In other words it is far more than folk stories of leprechauns and fairies in the woods. There are hierarchies of spiritual energies residing within the earth, largely ignored by the mystical community at large, since angelic hierarchies are easier to perceive. The long "Celtic" sagas still residing in the Irish psyche are testament both to the incredible gift of story-telling this nation once relied on in its daily life, and to the intimate knowledge the seannachies (story-tellers) had of invisible realms, that they expressed in terms of their familiar natural world.

When early Christians came to Ireland, the narrative faculty was still used liberally in the culture at large. A hermit would have been deeply in touch with nature, and the oral tradition was the only means of spreading his or her word. The placing of holy people on the western seaboard of Europe in places like Scotland, Portugal and particularly Ireland enabled a flowering of nature-based Christianity that matched well the spiritual energies afforded by that region. By contrast, in the Churches of the Middle East, the angelic hierarchies became the focal point of study over a long period of time.

This Celtic connection with nature spirits as evidenced in ancient prayers (4) is not what the later Church of Rome had in mind for spreading its own brand of Christianity. In the early centuries of Roman Christianity, the Church and State attempted to sever this blending with nature religion by labelling it heretical. Yet this way of thinking never disappeared entirely. The early Christian pioneers in Celtic areas were set apart from the old Druid religion but did not reject it either. To a universally revered quality of Christic love they brought an altruistic new dynamic to the table: recognition of the divine spark in nature, as well as in each person. This essential inter-connectivity between all sentient beings was a quality that the mystery schools and certain sects such as the Essenes had revered. It resurfaced in the early Celtic saints.

In keeping with the cycle of the pentagram and its qualities, we explore in this chapter the pioneering spirit inherent in the wood element by considering the lives of the early Christian saints of the Burren, and how they interacted with the land. Their lives were bound up with the elements and the energies associated with them that I will touch on throughout this book. I will also focus on the group of early Christians called the Culdees as they seem crucial the theme.

The Burren is a land bordered by the Atlantic to the west and the Shannon to the south. The Shannon is the main river in the west of Ireland, identified by experienced dowser Alana Moore as bearing a female serpentine energy along its centre. Siannan is the name for a granddaughter of the sea god Mananann. (Interestingly the name "Senan" for the local estuarine saint, born allegedly on 4/3/488, bears a close resemblance to the name Siannan. As is often the case with ecclesiastical names, they can echo those of regional gods and goblins.)

With the older rounded hills of the Slieve Aughtys to the east and the plains of fiercely tribal east Galway to the north, the Burren was not an ancient centre of pilgrimage and retreat until early Christian times. The early wanderer saints appear to have favoured long sojourns in the Burren and the adjacent Aran Isles, for there is by far the greatest density of ancient ecclesiastical settlements of all types here in Clare and the Burren, compared with other parts of Ireland. Among the island trio, Iniseer shares the same underlying rock formation as the Burren. The softer limestone rocks of Iniseer and the Burren are more feminine in character than the islands slightly to the north, which are underlain with harder rocks as found in most of mainland County Galway across the bay. Collectively the Burren and its western isles was a fertile ground for the imagination to take hold.

The Aran Isles "became to the adjacent West of Ireland what the great missionary settlement on the Island of Iona under St Columba's became at first to the mainland of Scotland"(5). They became associated in myths with perilous sea voyages, in which courageous monks reached blessed faraway isles, only after suffering many trials and tribulations. The mythical isles described bore a markedly other-worldly quality to them, a quality that reigned in the Celtic mythology of pre-Christian times. Man's ability to shift from one reality to another was an acceptable quality then, and in some ways we are coming full circle as a society now. Gradually more of us are realising that perception is determined by many factors, and we accept that we shape our reality according to how we perceive. Looking back it seems that these mythical voyages were created as aids to meditation, in which the islands and other events leading up to their discovery became symbols for various interior qualities or states of being. The monks would invariably encounter such states in contemplative prayer. These fascinating sea myths were known as immrams, and at least one of them comes into play in the making of this book and will be discussed in a later chapter.

The saints of the early centuries wandered over large swathes of land in Ireland, often en route to one or other centre of learning of excellence. Oft times they sailed to Scotland too. Place names and architectural clues supply scant though tantalising evidence of their sea journeys between both countries. The ley lines that I will feature in later chapters not only traverse land but also sea beds. In my own lifetime seasoned sailors have confided in me, admitting that they can detect lines of light or energy when at sea for protracted lengths of time. I believe that it is these lines that early saints such as Brendan and Columba sailed along, as they travelled to foreign lands to continue their missionary activities. It can be quite engaging to trace their travels, many of which occurred in the fifth and sixth centuries when they walked and sailed vast distances.

I would like to present a recent case study I made of St Creich as an example of how widely these saints travelled:

St Creich/Mac Creiche circa 440-510 seems to be associated with both Scotland and Ireland. He stayed on Holy Island in Lough Derg on the Shannon river in East Clare. Gerard Madden who wrote "Holy Island: Island of the Churches" is the local ferryman now. He tells us of a legend that hails from pagan times, when trees were sacred. An angel had bid St Creich to leave his home on Holy Island, where there was a tree called Tilia, whose juice could flow into a vessel and fill it. Its liquor tasted of honey, and yet it was as heady as wine. Creich was so fond of the liquor he was reluctant to follow the angel's later bidding to leave the pleasant islet.

The presence of such a fertile tree denotes the island was balanced in abundant earth energies. Certainly I dowsed many leys on the island one afternoon, when I visited with the ferryman. I am particularly fond of Holy Island also known as Inis Cealtra in East Clare where St Creich lived. It is said that an underground passage links this serene island on Lough Derg with Scattery Island in the mouth of the Shannon. How interesting that when I dowsed Inis Cealtra, I sensed and plotted a strong serpentine presence on it. I had not heard that there is a strong serpent energy passing down the Shannon that would pass through Scattery. Often, dowsing reveals certain aspects of the whole which our normal everyday minds bypass. What springs to mind at first when one is dowsing might make no sense, but later a legend or a piece of information will crop up that somehow lends substance to what is discerned while dowsing.

The feast day of Creich is the same as the festival of Crom Dubh, a most ancient pagan diety who was associated with dragons and snakes, who represent deep ley lines. This strongly suggests that Creich originally associated with the pagan religion! Crom Dubh was a John Barleycorn-like dark god of the fruits of the earth, whose lighter counterpart is Lugh of the Celtic Lughnassa festival. His feast day fell on the Sunday nearest the start of August which often would have coincided with Garland Sunday which fell on the last Sunday in July. Garland Sunday, a unique and popular festival, was celebrated with great revelry in the Liscannor area until recent times. Locals enjoyed their only day out in the year with a trip to the sands at Lahinch! Few attending might have appreciated its possible pagan origins. This family festival has even undergone a revival in current times! The local connection to Creich is strengthened by the fact that he led a shoreline school on the edge of Liscannnor, at the south end of the Burren (presumably after he left Holy Island upon the angel's bidding). St Creich offers a splendid example of the two religions gently colliding. It is more than likely that Creich taught the old nature religion alongside the new teachings of Christ - this attitude would makes him a veritable Culdee, those early Christians who bridged the old Druid ways with the new religion of Christianity.

A later church dedicated to St Creich on the same spot in the twelfth century was known as Kilmacreehy (kil means church). Here the church displays a dragon or large cat with pointed ears on one of its lintels though when I visited it, much of the carving had been destroyed. Legends of St Creich feature dragons, a theme shared by the pagan god Crom Dubh.

As a place name, Creich is fairly common in Scotland although no one knows its exact meaning. For years I had known of a church built perhaps in the fourteenth century in a pleasant hamlet called Creich, overlooking the banks of the sacred river Tay in Fife. Close by there are Iron Age hut remains. Interestingly the church was named St Devenick, after a mysterious figure who lived somewhere between 300 and 600 CE, who is said to have been one of the last missionaries to leave St Ninian's teaching monastery at Whithorn in Galloway, in order to convert the northern Picts to Christianity. St Ninian's life spanned the fourth and fifth centuries. His school was closely connected with the Culdees. Ninian taught many missionaries who sailed the short distance from Ireland.

The church at Creich lies quite close to St Andrews, where there was a very early Culdee church on the rocks, known as St Magdalene on the Rocks. Mary Magdalene figures strongly in the wider Culdee picture. In the late eleventh century Queen Margaret of Scotland sought out the Culdee places for quiet and contemplation, and two ferry ports were built to transport her from Edinburgh to Fife, so she could specifically visit the church on the rocks at St Andrews. This queen became a saint and is a most interesting character. I always sensed that the site at Creich could have been connected to the Magdalene church in St Andrews.

By 1330 the church at Creich was associated in monastic documents with St Serf, another very early dragon-slaying saint who is said to have reared St Mungo in the sixth century. St Mungo founded Glasgow. St Serf and St Creich shared similar hagiographies, slaying dragons and such like. The nearby Cistercian monastery of Lindores was associated with the church at Creich in the Middle Ages. This order was closely connected to the Knights Templar in Scottish history and I have often noted these early medieval knights and monks settled in old Culdee areas.

Creich can also be found, as a place name, at the tip of the Hebridean Isle of Mull, where an old church stands hard by the Sound of Iona, a small stretch of sea that separates Mull from that special isle. Both Mull and Iona have strong Culdee connections. They are most sacred places. Finally Creich is a large highland parish on a very long inlet westwards of the eastern coastline in northern Scotland (Sutherland) where Devenick lived too! Could it be that Devenick and Creich was one and the same person? Perhaps the Picts knew Creich by the alternative name of Devenick?

In the Domesday Book of 1086 the surnames Creich and Creic are mentioned, both of which are derived from old Welsh (a Celtic tongue named "Byrthonic" in Victorian times). This was the language spoken by the saints that Ninian trained. The word Creic means rock. The name suggests that Creich was an important figure in the early Christian missionary movement, and certainly places associated with him impart tremendous peace and a sense of timelessness. Since Creich is mostly associated with coastal or deep river sites it seems likely he sailed around the coasts of Scotland and Ireland founding small Culdee Christian settlements, and hence his association with both countries.

Who were the Culdees as a movement or sect? Their existence is more or less accepted but the scant data for the dating of this movement varies widely. Their early churches may have been built of clay not stone, and therefore would not have lasted until now. Their beehive cells of stone did last in places like Skellig Michael off the coast of Kerry, but many have disappeared too. Two beehive cells on Bishops Island in the river Shannon were recorded by Rev White (6) in 1893. Bishops Island translates as "island of the fasting bishop". Later on when these early Christians grew in number their beehives gave way to small stone cells with curving roofs, partly to accommodate the followers. These were "intermediate between the Beehive structure, with the pointed oratory on the one hand, and the cathedral and abbey on the other" (7). Such an oratory with rounded corners, a simple stone altar of slab, a bench of stones all round the interior walls, and a grave at the west end for receiving ashes of the dead stood at Sladoo in the heart of the Burren (near Carron), and was recorded in 1878 (8). However by 1900, when T. J. Westropp compiled his archaeological survey of Clare, there was no sign of the altar and the church appears to have gone into rapid decline. This is indicative of how by modern times traces of many early churches were lost in the Burren. Moreover, most early Irish records were destroyed, so it is difficult to rely on written accounts from centuries later.

The best Culdee reference book is Isobel Hill Elder's book "Celt Druid and Culdee" written in 1938, that extensively references early Greek and Roman travel writers to the British Isles. Their travel reports indicate there were pockets of Christians living in what are now mostly isolated rural hamlets. The reports do not proffer a reason for the existence of these groups. Perhaps to them the reason was obvious. It might have come about when local people went to work for the Roman Empire, returning to their pagan homelands with the new beliefs they had encountered and adopted whilst working in the Middle East. Christianity had no rigid structure until the Council of Nicea met in 325, whereby the Nicene Creed was created. This emphatically ruled out the beliefs of Arius of the Church of Antioch, who practised in Alexandria. The Culdees appear to have followed his doctrine that believed Jesus was born by the power of God's word as a man, rather than always existing within the Trinity. The Council in the fourth century ruled out a wide range of beliefs in favour of what later became the Church of Rome, but were only partially successful in their implementation. The Culdees continued. I imagine that many of these believers moved to the western fringes of Europe to avoid persecution. In 664 the Synod of Whitby in Yorkshire tried to subdue the "Celtic Church" but it continued in the Celtic fringe of England bordering the Irish Sea (9), Meanwhile in Ireland and Scotland, it continued more or less freely until the late eleventh century. Early texts from Ireland serve to illustrate their close links with a wide spectrum of Middle Eastern texts. More suggestive evidence arose when an eighth century religious book was discovered in a bog close to the old ecclesiastical centre of Birr in County Offaly in 2006. The Fadden More Psalter was written in vellum sections whose cover was lined with Middle Eastern papyrus! Lapis lazuli created the blue pigmentation on the decorative pages. Such a gem was not local! Culdean literary books and habits lead a writer to conclude in the latter half of the twelfth century that they were from Africa and of Judaic beliefs. As part of his investigation he examined life in the Orkney Islands to the northeast of Scotland in the 1400s, observing that the Papae wore white robes in priest-like fashion(10). Harald Boehkle believes these Papae were Irish monks, and descriptions of them in the Orkney manuscript bear close resemblance to what we know of the Culdees. Those monks were also welcome in the court of Charlemagne, where their wisdom was much appreciated. Alcuin a court theologian complained that the "Egyptians had replaced the Latins at court". (11)

According to some historians, the Culdee (12) monks could marry and own their own land. They served the populace by administering herbal remedies they prepared. Their homes were beehive-shaped mud or stone cells and they lived in clusters thus. The beehive is an ancient structure which spread beyond its origins in the Eastern Mediterranean region. In ancient Egypt, they were built traditionally to commemorate the reliquary chest that housed the head of the god Osiris. For them a beehive shape represented the collective wisdom of humanity. The ancient Ethiopian Church in Jerusalem to this day consists of such dwellings, poised poignantly on the roof area of the Church of the Holy Sepulchre.

When a group of Culdees grew beyond the size of twelve people they splintered off and began a new cluster group, rather than grow into a larger community which would have lent itself to hierarchical structures. Judging by reliable travel accounts the hallmarks of these special groups were equality, humility and a wish to serve in the name of Christ. Perhaps unsurprisingly, the descriptions of their lifestyle closely matched those of the Essenes, an esoteric sect that Jesus purportedly spent a lot of time with in the Middle East prior to his better-known three year mission, recorded in the New Testament. Along with a host of eclectic religious groups, the Essenes had to flee Jerusalem when the Romans sacked Jerusalem. Isobel Hill Elder presents a solid argument for the fact that the name "Culdees" meant "strangers from afar" and that they were closely linked to the Essenic communities in the Mediterranean area whence they came by boat. The Essenes were sworn to the utmost secrecy so this might also explain why the Culdees left little trace of who they were.

From a historical perspective, Jerusalem holds the key to understanding the lineage to which the Culdees seem to belong. In his excellently researched book "Templar Nation", Freddy Silva goes to great lengths to explain the connections between a few significant groups who occupied key sites in Jerusalem just prior to the start of the Crusades. Again the Essenes figure as a salient force. Although they were long gone by the time the Knights of the Holy Sepulchre, the Priory of Sion, the Cistercians and Knights Templar all converged on Jerusalem, Silva painstakingly has traced the lineage of the these four co-dependent groups to the Essenes (13). These medieval groups shared the same moral values, vows, and outward signs in clothing and cultural practices as the Essenes. To this melting pot I can add the Culdees, whose lifestyles echoed that of the Essenes, within a much shorter time span than that of their medieval counterparts.

The Essenes left their knowledge in scrolls secreted in vaults on the Temple of the Mount in Jerusalem, a site whose history I was unaware of at the time I dowsed it, finding it to be extremely potent. Above lies the tomb of David and above that still are the rooms where Jesus is reputed to have held his Last Supper. Over the years I have learnt to trust my dowsing skills and in later chapters will explain the art in greater depth, relating some stories to indicate how fortuitous a path this interest has lead me at times. In a range of esoteric and Judaic literature it is widely believed that Jesus and his family were members of the Nasoreans, who were similar initiates or even identical to the Essenes. John the Baptist was their religious leader, though their roots go back to Egypt. The Nasoreans were in turn part of a wider sect, named after secret knowledge, called the Mandeans. The search is endless in where it leads us in the complex culture that thrived in the times Jesus lived.

I mention the above details because the Cistercians and Knights Templar also travelled to Scotland and Ireland (although in Ireland the Knights Templar did not last long thanks to Papist zeal, and the Cistercians were successfully ordered to change their outlook to a conformist Roman Catholic one after about fifty short years, partly as they had no surviving secular brotherhood in the form of the Knights Templar to continue their mission). In contrast, both groups flourished for centuries in Scotland.

There may have been a necessary counterpart action provided by the two groups who moved to Ireland. Here I am talking on a spiritual and soul level rather than a physical one. We already know these groups were associated with secret knowledge whose purpose was to establish Heaven on Earth. There was an even more obscure agenda that does not hit headlines because it is not sensational enough. I would maintain that those groups of Cistercians and long-gone Knights Templar who sailed along the Atlantic seaboard to Cork, the Shannon estuary, Galway and Sligo were also linking in with an earlier tradition held in Ireland. They were following in the footsteps of those Culdees who worked with the elemental rather than angelic energies. Ireland has always had a special role in protecting the twilight zone of the Sidhe or elementals as my later chapter on the subject will indicate. It is harder to contact this realm and requires the quiet discipline of the ascetic who chooses to live in relative isolation. This path is complementary to those working with the angelic hierarchies, about which much has been written.

In terms of the aforementioned earth grids that I have studied under William Buehler, the UK and Ireland as a whole carries a "Grail" consciousness. The UK provides an umbrella structure for the manifestation of the Grail Cup, and accordingly processes knowledge more consciously than Ireland. Meanwhile and of no less importance, Ireland is represented by the communion host itself, innocently awaiting its own consumption. She holds the key to subconscious energies connected with the divine feminine and the creative principle. Perhaps this principle is portrayed, or at least symbolically represented, in those sheela-na-gigs who grace the early medieval churches. Here then at the edge of Europe was a force that lay hidden from the more masculine Roman church didactics.

Silva, as mentioned, before traces the route that links the Essenes to later powerful sects. He also vindicates them as a spiritual tour de force that worked with adepts, who were initiated into universal secret knowledge. It seems highly likely that the Essenic way of life was transferred to Britain and Ireland in small pockets of Culdee /strangers who in turn converted some local people wherever they settled, for travel reports inform us of their existence. While the Culdees inherited a rich knowledge of the archangels and the higher heavens, they now embraced working intimately with the devic kingdoms/lower heavens. This bringing together of two separate knowledge streams was very significant. The Pagan faith was waning when the Culdees appeared on the scene. In terms of the evolution of consciousness, Paganism lacked focus or appreciation of the new Christ energy and inevitably waned as a mass religion. On the other hand, the Culdees embraced the new consciousness as taught by Christ. I view it that the Christ event was a cosmic mark in mankind's evolution, and yet it is only now rooting itself: people are starting to embody his simple message that they have the power to transform their lives, and exponentially develop human wisdom and love. In fact, sacred knowledge once held in mystery schools and sects is giving rise to direct experience more and more.

During a twenty year sojourn in Scotland I found many old Culdee settlements that were placed on strong ley lines, and it reminded me of the way that Aboriginal cultures move around and use places with positive energies as temporary abodes. Early Churches were often built over these small monastic sites. In Ireland, extant research into the Culdees is unfortunately very limited. I was told when enquiring in antiquarian bookstores that there were very little written records of them, though the oral culture still acknowledged them. This is understandable since their whole ethos was passed on orally and little documentation has survived in later times, due to religious persecution.

By contrast in Scotland, Fiontullach (nee Fiona Davidson) is a female hermetic of the Culdee tradition who continues a long oral teaching as passed on from her predecessor. She is the first person to inherit the knowledge without belonging to the bloodline that harboured it. She calls her group the Ceili Dei, meaning Companions of God. Her work is very rare, valuable and grace-filled. Teachings are experiential rather than theoretical. I shall give an example here, of what occurred when working with her in my workshops on earth grids in Roslin, Scotland. While visiting Roslin Glen in small groups we used to chant the ancient Culdee chants. The birds often responded in extraordinary ways when we were seated outside in nature.

Once after an hour of beautiful chanting in a deep cave we emerged and one participant took a picture of me outside the entrance. When she had the film developed, a strong wide beam of orange and golden light was seen coming from the cave, passing directly through my heart region and middle torso. Margaret McCallum, who took the photograph, was a medium in her own right, and had many professional photographers study the film reel for accidental light entry and so forth. All remarked that the light was not due to mechanical failure of any kind. The photos either side of this picture held no such light and it was verified as authentic. Neither am I used to being photographed in such a light in the glen!

From my own understanding and from listening to the soft teachings of Fiontullach, it seems to me that experiencing the divine Christ essence was the main ethos of the Culdees. For them, Christ was soft and female in quality, and existed in all matter, and above all, in nature. The spiritual world indeed pervades everything, if we have but eyes to see and hearts to notice.

Historians categorized the Culdees as a Gnostic group that existed in the centuries after Constantine's Roman Church had gained supremacy of faith to the exclusion of others. This change in direction followed the decisions taken at the aforementioned Council of Nicea in modern-day Turkey. The Council of Nicea seemed to favour the creation of doctrine and dogma, above personal direct experience of the divine. Such an attitude was the antithesis of Culdee and Essenic practices. As an outward excuse for dismantling groups that did not adhere to their way of thinking, the Council of Nicea set the date for celebrating Easter according to a new Roman method of

calculation, and those sects who did not comply were naturally marginalized. The fate of many sects was effectively sealed. The word "sect" has negative connotations now, but in reality both the Essenes and the Culdees were slightly hidden groups whose ways were non-confrontational and peaceful; studying esoteric texts, practising daily meditation that emphasized inner experience above all, and thereby shying away from dogma.

The Culdees survived into the medieval period in northern England and Scotland. Even in the fifteenth century there were separate aisles set aside for Culdee worship in St Andrews Cathedral and Durham Cathedral. In Ireland and many areas of Britain, safe from the constant prying eyes of the Continental bishops, the old nature-loving Christ-centred faith remained as a viable alternative. I sensed that keenly when visiting the Aran isle of Inisheer, many years ago.

I would like to relate an anecdote that adds fuel to my theory about the Culdees being present very early in this part of Ireland. One day while on Iniseer I was pondering on the early Christian tradition of the island. I was sitting on the edge of a field looking out to sea towards the neighbouring island of Inismaan. In my hand lay a book I was reading about the history of

Armenia. Philip Marsden's travelogue The Crossing Place led me to believe that there was a link between the Armenian Christians and the Celtic Christians. I hurriedly wrote a letter to his editor since I had no address for him. A few weeks later, I received a letter back from Philip, written in an air of slight consternation. He told me that he had been staying on the isle of Inismaan at the same time I wrote him my letter, and that he had reached the same conclusion regarding the historical links between these two groups of early Christians. He too sensed that the early Jerusalem Church had been active in the Burren. However he said he had visited the Armenian cathedral complex in Jerusalem, and realised that without being able to decipher their ancient books (they were one of the first nations to take to Gutenberg's printing press!) the potential for research was limiting.

A year or so later I visited the same city and at the gates of the Armenian community was cordially met by the Archdeacon of the Armenian cathedral, who gave me a grand tour of his walled compound. He insisted on giving me a branch of olives from the very tree that Jesus had been bound to when beaten. I felt uneasy with the gesture but tactfully accepted his gift from the protected tree. The congenial clergyman was curious to know how Rosslyn Chapel in Scotland was doing since I lived in the village beside it. This was decades before it shot to fame in the Da Vinci Code book. He admitted he knew there was a strong link between the Celtic Church and the Armenian Church. Perhaps pockets of early Christians had moved west I wondered, having at one point been of the same early Jerusalem church. I slowly over the years began to realise why I sensed this strong connection between the far western outposts of Christianity and the heart of Jerusalem.

Some years later, I was contacted by a research student in Edinburgh to discuss the roots of the Celts. He believed they hailed from the Altai mountains – he said that he had discovered local shamanic practices and visual rock art that bore close resemblances to the patterns of the Celts. I did muse on the fact that wondrous tales of the early Celtic saints seemed to reflect current shamanic practices in Siberia. I then discovered that Philip Marsden had diverted his attention away from finding Celtic links with the Armenian Church to researching shamanic practices from the Siberian steppes, close to the Altai Mountains! To me this theory of shared distant roots in shamanism felt truthful and I had long learnt to trust my instincts. The Altai Mountains in Siberia may well be the starting point for all epic journeys of the Celts, as we know them today.

Later still I read that the Celts had travelled across in two waves to Britain and Ireland. No one really knew from whence they came prior to a split, east of the Mediterranean somewhere. One wave came through Switzerland and gave rise to La Tenne culture, famous for its richly adorned objects. This wave who traditionally settled outside of Ireland may have also settled in the Burren around Kilnaboy. Their language used the double "L" and in the Burren there are isolated instances of this occurring at the start of place names (e.g. Llaungraffanavrankagh)

The use of the double "L", along with the use of the "p" sound, was spoken by the tribes who settled in Brittany, Wales and Cornwall. Hence "Map" or "Ap" meant "son of". By contrast the Godelic Celts settled In Ireland, the Isle of Man and later Scotland. Their "son of" read as "Mac" but earlier the sound was perceived as a "q" for which English had no equivalent consonant without following it by a "u". From Victorian times this variation in languages has been used to identify two distinct settling patterns of the Celts.

It is quite extraordinary to contemplate a separate wave of Celtic reaching Ireland contrary to the normally perceived migratory pattern. However the "Dean of Lismore" in remote Glen Lyon in the sixteenth century wrote that a small band of these "p Celts" reached the Hebrides and parts of the Scottish Highlands, where a distinct tongue had been spoken, centuries before the "q Celts" of the Dal Riada sept expanded from Ireland into the south west of Scotland (14). These Celts were perceived as special emissaries with a culture of their own. Meanwhile the far more commonly acknowledged Dal Riada were part of a larger migratory wave from North Africa who had settled in Ireland, as well-documented by film-maker Bob Quinn. Quinn drew popular attention to the close links between the Arab and Celtic language and cultural practices such as singing.. The barely acknowledged early presence of p Celts in the Perthshire Highlands followed through to it being the last remaining Gaelic speaking area on the Mainland of Scotland. Their customs were most unusual, and included a daily greeting in the name of St Martin rather than God, and other fascinating ritual references to the Middle East, offering the strongest remaining clues to the possibility of a very small but early exodus of Christians to the western fringes of Europe. Since the early Irish saints also abided in this valley, it is worth noting the link.

After this long introduction to the Culdees, I now would like to home in on their possible presence in the Burren. The Culdees were drawn to places that were deeply elemental, meaning the nature spirits, or elementals, inhabited their lonely spots. Often all we have is a place name to go on as all traces of their habitation have weathered away. Even visiting a Culdee site today imparts a deep sense of their presence, to anyone who is sensitive to vibrations. It is quite feasible that male and female monks of the Culdee tradition found their way to remote parts of the Burren in the early centuries after Christ, or at least in the decades before St Patrick's mission. There seems to be no pilgrim tradition in the Burren prior to the monks setting foot there in the sixth century. Given the Burren was devoid of earlier pilgrim rituals, the pioneer monks were able to start with a clean slate. They chose their sites for prayer with only the prevailing sweet influence of nature. The Burren to this day has a wide profusion of flowers and variety of butterflies. This would have suited the Culdee tradition of living in harmony with nature, as evidenced in accounts that survive from documents written in the Middle Ages. These were the first records of a group whose traditions were strictly oral. Accounts of their lives that had been passed down orally over the centuries altered with the establishment of written records, and probably marked the start of their demise, that seemed to last from the thirteenth to the fifteenth centuries.

The Burren saints would have found its stony desert an appropriate environment in which to emulate the ways of St Anthony of Pispir who preached in the Egyptian desert in the fourth century. He in turn influenced St Martin de Tours, in the so-called tradition of the "Desert Fathers". It called for a life of purity and self-imposed austerity. St Martin influenced Culdee saints such as the dragon-slaying St Serf (362-432), one of the first recorded saints in Scotland, where the word "desert" is known as "dysart", a dialect word. When used as a place name, some believe "Dysart" refers to a past settlement of beehive cells, since the earliest monks lived their hermetic lives in beehive cells. In the Bathgate Hills to the west of Edinburgh, the late gentleman Jack Smith of the Order of St John wrote convincingly in a small booklet entitled "Torphicen" of the presence of such beehives in multiple local locations including Dysart, an area by the river Avon. He viewed the early inhabitants as dwellers of the desert, simultaneously calling them Culdees. Meanwhile Dysart in Fife is close by Kirkcaldy (meaning Church of the Culdees). Others interpret Dysart as a Celtic word Dys-ard meaning Height of God. Others still say it comes from Latin denoting the fasting place of a Holy Man. All these interpretations point to a similar theme - they denote a place associated with being close to the divine.

Crossing the water to Ireland, in Clare on the landward side of the Burren lies the small village of Corofin. In its pretty environs lies a well-preserved castle with a nearby Celtic high cross. This is the quiet hamlet of Dysart O'Dea, which allegedly means God's Desert! Its twelfth century church exhibits a French style of ornamentation indicating it was a place or learning and culture, and it stands over a much earlier Christian settlement. As is often the case with old ecclesiastical settlements in Ireland, the remnants of an ancient round tower stands close to the present church. Quite close to Dysart O'Dea lies another remote and charming church ruins: Rath Blamaic overlooks Loch Raha which features in the next chapter on dragon energies. Here one of Ireland's most enigmatic sheela-na-gig lies inverted on an eleventh century lintel. This classical carving of a female figure with her full genitalia exposed is grappling with two dragons. This surely makes her a strong contender for hot favourite among the sheela-na-gig spotters! I learnt from a farmer that another round tower used to stand in the adjacent field, but was sadly demolished entirely by his late relations. I also read, in the local history library in Ennis, that there were other round towers on the ridge overlooking the site - I will be writing extensively about the possible meaning and functions of these special round towers later. Around Dysart O'Dea there are twenty five ancient monuments worth visiting. Unobtrusively standing off the road between Kilfenora and Kilnaboy, one of Ireland's most enigmatic monuments has to be noted. Known as the Tau cross, it is an unusual T- shaped cross stone with two long heads carved either end looking skywards. Stylised hands grasp one another in the middle. Once it stood on top of a rocky outcrop, and a good replica has replaced it. The original stone (now in Corofin museum) appears to have functioned as a boundary marker.

According to Canon Dwyer writing in 1878, there used to be three boundary crosses in the area (15). Very near the cross stands a large fort, or caher, with a subterranean chamber - typically people still lived in these forts during the early Christian period. The Tau cross also features on a twelfth century cross in Kilfenora Cathedral, an important cathedral nearby. This was undoubtedly the first diocese for a large clan as there are many large forts close by. St Fachnan who founded the church is depicted there on an ornamental cross slab, wearing a frontal tonsure as used by the Culdees. He is holding a chalice close to him in the style of the early church, and he is

wearing an eastern-style tunic. One carving among the collection of crosses shows a monk or priest bearing a Tau cross. Bishops of the Egyptian Church carried such T-formed croziers.

The boundary cross on the roadside carries two main aspects in its symbolism: the double head and the Tau shape. First considering the Tau symbol, we can look at ancient Jewish mysticism from which Christianity sprang anew. The Tau is the last letter in the Hebrew alphabet. It synthesizes all the letters in the Hebrew alphabet, all of which carried deep inner meanings, and therefore it is very complex in meaning. In Jewish initiation ceremonies, you receive a Tau or Tav each time you pass an initiation. In the Reshel system, a Christo-Judaic system concerned with inner mysteries, the Tav holds a numerical value of 400, and is characterized by an equal-armed cross. It is indeed a high master number with many functions.

The Tau is an enigmatic Egyptian symbol with many possible meanings including well-being, immortality and protection. Moses is said to have used the Tau for healing. When one of the Desert Fathers, St Anthony, adopted the cross he became famous for good health. After St Anthony's time St Francis used the cross to protect his workers from contracting diseases. If disease was spreading through the countryside in Clare this might have been a talisman. Certainly there used to be local leper colonies in the vicinity of this cross, and there is a leper's squint window in the old parish church at Kilnaboy close by.

The Gauls perceived that the Tau cross stood for Thor's hammer as an instrument of life and fecundity. The local saint Inghine Baoith (daughter of Baoith) of Kilnaboy has local connotations with fertility. She founded a nunnery at Kilnaboy in the sixth century. Her name later became shortened to Innerwee. If the Tau cross near Kilnaboy was associated with the desert fathers then it might have been carved with the theme of healing in mind; in the sixth century the local nuns no doubt were practised herbalists. Positioned on a hill overlooking the approach to the nunnery, could it be that the Tau cross symbolically acted as a form of protector for this fertile region? This may sound far-fetched, but in times when there were few distractions, stone cutters and stone masons of high standing were familiar with working intent into their craft. The creation and exact placement of monuments and symbols was a form of acceptable magic well into early Masonic times. Craftsmen learnt not just a craft but an accompanying inner philosophy, and working with stone was an accomplished job that afforded them esteemed positions within society.

Looking at the Tau cross' unusual feature of the double head, if the stone is of the later medieval period there may have been an informed cultural link with France that inspired the creation of the cross. Double heads were commonly depicted on medieval crosiers carved in the locality of Roquepertuse in south-east France. This would make perfect sense in the context of there being a local medieval church at Kilnaboy and an important school of masons based at the nearby cathedral at Kilfenora, where some of the free standing crosses also display the Tau cross.

However, symbols appear at spots for invisible reasons too. In the time of the Knights Templar, they possessed an array of mystic symbols. The human head represented the Earth, or rather the sentient aspect of Earth now generally known as Gaia. When a symbol splits into two it indicates an intensifying of the quality appertaining to it, according to mystic geometer and scholar William Buehler (who invented the term Reshel from his study of early Hebrew letters). In the proto-Sinaitic glyphs the Resh was depicted as a profile of a human head. The head or Resh symbolised the control point within a spiritual programme. A double head, in the esoteric symbolism of the Reshel system that I studied for many years, indicates that an intended spiritual programme in the area is highly active and intensified. The only other double headed stone I know of in Ireland is located on Boa Island, in upper Lough Derg in Fermanagh, where the style differs somewhat. The island cemetery is very peaceful there.

Kilnaboy Church was built on the nunnery site around the twelfth century and added onto later. Another round tower stands in ruins adjacent, and a bedraggled looking sheela-na-gig splays her legs over the south doorway of the church, repeating the theme of fertility and reminding us of the role fertility plays in all our lives. The western gable of the church hints at further esoteric links. A large pattern of a two armed cross, known as the Cross of Lorraine, is incorporated into the structure of the wall. Lorraine as a region stems from the ancient kingdom of Lotharingia, and by introduction to the topic, King Loth of the Lothians in Scotland hailed from this region. Interestingly in West Lothian a well-preserved boundary stone to the east of the preceptory of the Knights of St John in Torphicen bears the Cross of Lorraine. The Cross was used by Joan of Arc when she went into battle and it also has connections with the Crusades. There would have been knights passing through West Lothian, and the Knights Templar are said to have lived there and surrendered their lands to the Knights of St John. What knights might have ridden through Kilnaboy though? Did the Templars briefly visit the area, as they used to restock with supplies along the west coast of Ireland from time to time?

There has to be some reason behind the decision to construct a wall that uniquely incorporates the Cross of Lorraine. Perhaps there was a Gaulish influence in both the erection of the Tau cross and the Cross of Lorraine? The cross was generally adopted to stand for the pilgrim route to Jerusalem. Some believe it signifies the church held a relic of the cross Jesus died on. This would have made it an important church to travel to. I believe the area was long recognized for its fertility and was long associated with fertility rites. As time wore on it became an important Christian site. Interestingly the Merovingians ruled part of Gaul in the Celtic period, and this dynasty was perceived as demi gods in the time immediately before the golden age of Celtic saints. Kilnaboy and the Tau cross are part of an ongoing mystery for archaeologists to solve.

Moving further into the interior of the Burren, there is a small ruined church near Carron village that is dedicated to another of the early Christian saints; St Cronan. (In Tuamgraney in East Clare, the church dedicated to him there has an unusual south door that looks more typical of an Egyptian temple door, with slanting vertical jambs and a very thick lintel above. Tuamgraney is known to be one of the earliest oratories in Clare.) In the oratory of St Cronan's in Carron, there is a holy well beside a man-made unexcavated mound. There once was a cross there too. Near the church are two reliquaries shaped like miniature houses with sloping roofs. These again are quite rare and denote the pilgrim tradition of revering the bones of a saint. Like so many of the tiny early churches in the Burren, the dimensions are about thirteen feet by twenty one feet. This was clearly intended on behalf of the builders. It creates a golden mean rectangle (calculated by using the golden mean ratio of 1:1.618). These classical proportions, when applied to buildings, can help ensure harmony and promote stillness. Whenever a chapel or temple is constructed to these proportions, the person standing inside will feel more readily elevated to higher states of mind. It is one of the reasons there were so few windows, as the building was no doubt designed for meditation, inward reflection and prayer. Views after all can distract! Perhaps it was not designed for celebrating Mass for the masses... the churches in this region are made of the local stone which is oolitic rather than normal limestone. This type of rock contains particles of sand (quartz) trapped in egg-shaped stones that were sealed together at high intensity. The building can be programmed much in the same way a computer can! (16) It can be instructed to harness the telluric energies thus. Interestingly, this was the first site of the early Christian period I headed for when I moved to Ireland. I also wonder if there are underground currents running through the site. In the final chapter, we read of how rushing water is electrically charged. When standing inside a building with fast underground currents, this can positively affect the person's psychic abilities.

St Colman, whose centre was on the north side of the Burren, is the most fascinating saint in the region. He lived in the sixth century too and his life story displays similar characteristics to many of the Culdee saints. Cousin to King Guaire who founded two settlements at Gort and Kinvara (where a later castle remains), St Colman was one of the great Celtic saints of the west of Ireland where he founded Kilmacduagh, the foremost monastery in the west. Thus began a long lineage. In 1152 its diocese more or less matched those of the former kingdom of Hy Fiachrach Aidhne which his relatives ruled in the sixth century.

He was born near Kiltartan, in the vicinity of what would more than a thousand years later become Coole Park, the home of Lady Gregory, who together with WB Yeats and other instrumental thinkers revived national interest in Celtic mythology and culture in the nineteenth century. Back in the sixth century at the time Colman was due to be born, the High King of Connaught received a warning that he would become the most distinguished in his noble family, and so he ordered him to be drowned upon birth. Tying a heavy stone around his pregnant mother Rhinagh, they threw her into a deep pool nearby.... the stone miraculously floated on the waters, allowing Colman's birth to take place after all. This pool is likely to be the one that lies adjacent to Lord Gregory's grave - one of the most serene spots in the county. Yet the power of the waters here cannot be underestimated. Three underground rivers emerge here and the currents are strong and deep. In effect it is a triple spring. Thus one could claim significance to Colman's baptismal rite in a (significant) triple spring before he was even born! After his birth his mother secreted him away with the monks who reared and educated him, as there were already Christian enclaves in the immediate locality.

As a young ardent monk, Colman is said to have lived seven years in retreat at Kinalia below Eagle's Rock, without knowing that the cruel king who had tried to drown him was no more, and had been replaced by a kinder cousin known as "Guaire the Generous" who was in command of the area. When on full retreat Colman's sole mortal companions were a fly to mark the lines in his psalter, a mouse to turn the pages therein and a cockerel to wake him for early morning prayers. (The local church of Tierneevin charmingly displays these creatures and St Colman in a stained glass window.)

It is interesting that the saint chose a spot below the limestone cliffs to dwell. The electromagnetic properties of carbonaceous strata like limestone are powerful when water moves through them. There is water passing through the hermitage, helping to conduct the telluric energies (ground currents). Water passing through limestone increases the negative ions in the atmosphere. This serves to positively affect the spirit of place for meditation purposes. (It incidentally also results in increased plant growth and yield in general.)

Fluctuations in electro-magnetism produced, especially along areas where two types of land intersect, cause a condition they label "conductivity discontinuity" that has dramatic effects on the human brain. Also according to Burke and Halberg's research (17), fluctuations in heavier positive ions are produced along escarpments in the rock, and these can be powerful places to sit. There is a possibility that Kinalia displays these properties which would make it conducive to altered states of consciousness. Underlying water fluctuates in levels and directions throughout the year. This will in turn create changes in the telluric energies in the land. It is the fluctuations in the geomagnetic field that affect the production of chemicals made by the pineal gland. The gland is situated near the centre of our brain and is shaped like a pine-cone. Pinoline and serotonin interact to create a hallucinogen called DMT. So people living in places where the geomagnetic field can decrease in intensity are subject to experiencing psychic and shamanic states. There is also a fault line lying parallel to the cliffs a short distance away, and it is at the edges of fault lines that electromagnetic forces vary most.

St Colman's small oratory, a charming sanctuary in the hazel woods at the foot of limestone cliffs, contains some rudimentary altars upon which rounded pieces of shale were placed until recently. In the summer months, religious rites or "patterns" were performed using the two altars. The stones or votive offerings marked each round of penitence that a pilgrim would make on their hands and knees around the site! Such patterns were confined to holy places and holy wells, both of which are represented at Kinalia below Eagle's Rock. Apart from these simple altars, often with modern votive offerings placed upon them, we can see the cave where Colman is supposed to have lived and prayed, the well built downstream from a spring in the cliffs, the grave of his servant, and hoof-shaped and dish-shaped indentations on the rocky ground beyond. The latter relate to the legend "The Way of the Dishes".

This legend has it that early in the seventh century Colman and a small retinue of monks retired to fast and pray in the wilderness, as in the Culdee tradition of retiring to a desert. It was Lent and fasting was severe on the company of monks. One of them openly yearned for meat, and Colman out of pity for his fellow's suffering prayed. At the time, his cousin King Guaire was entertaining his guests at Dunguaire, his castle near Kinvara, when suddenly his entire feast of food took off into the air and started to travel speedily inland to the foot of the limestone cliffs where St Colman was so actively praying! Perhaps his pineal gland had been affected by fluctuations in the geomagnetic field - the gland's activity peaks late at night, a time when after fasting all day one becomes really hungry!

The courtiers started to chase their food on horseback and were terrified when they found their own feet and the hooves of their horses stuck fast in the rocks as they came close to Colman's retreat. After Colman successfully prayed for their release the local high king recognized the powers of his saintly cousin. The "servant" or monk had had his fill before the feast was returned, but the food was so rich it unfortunately killed him, and his grave lies nearby too!

King Guaire the Generous was delighted to be reunited with his long lost cousin, and in gratitude and recognition he granted him land on which to build a monastery. Upon hearing this news Colman immediately left his hermitage and walked on. To this day local farmers know the route taken, along which there are many ancient holy wells. Shortly Colman came upon the site now known as Kilmacduagh where he observed the pre-ordained sign he was waiting for; his girdle (or belt) fell to the ground at the spot where he was to build his monastery. It would be interesting to know where he wore his belt as the depositing of his belt might signify a chakra point on a ley line if we knew which chakra (energy centre) his belt lay over. Old archives record an even older monastic complex at Sheeaun ("hill of the fairies") a few miles away, where six of seven old buildings were traceable on the ground in 1940. I went to check the site with a friend, and after wandering through labyrinths of hazel thickets we found but glimpses remaining above the ground. Hazel scrub is the main vegetation cover over parts of the Burren. Interestingly this tree holds heat as does the limestone it grows above. Even when the bushes are bare and the frost is visible the branches can feel warm I have been told! This sings to me of some special spirit that resides in the species.

Many early monks are said to have known or worked with Colman, whose monastery was of great importance in the days before official diocese were formed. Rulers of monasteries were often respected for their oratorical and healing powers and Colman was no exception. The nearby town of Gort has the motto of "Home to the Stranger". Interestingly the Culdee monks in Scotland were called "strangers from afar" in Gaelic. Could it be that Colman, a widely recognized and revered monk, belonged to the Culdees, and this was why the name of the local town refers to his saintly movement? I think it probable. Another interesting speculation is that the "Way of the Dishes" also marks a ley line between the castle on the promontory in Kinvara Harbour and the hermitage at Kinalia. Interestingly a personal friend of mine Neil Casey once was walking on the heights above Kinalia when he found himself transported some distance in the twinkling of an eye. When he gave his account of the event later I felt he had "teleported". He told me he felt he had been following a ley line that connected what looked like cairns that had not been recorded. He may have entered into another dimension temporarily - I have known other completely sane people to experience similar things. For Neil, this was a first and he was quite excited!

When Kilmacduagh was founded in 610, there was no sign of all the ecclesiastical buildings that can be seen in ruins today. Colman's original cell is said to have lain to the east of the present cathedral, and there is a small stone structure within the graves in that area. A beautiful crozier that belonged to St Colman is on display in the Dublin Museum (Dept of Antiquities). After 1152, when diocese were founded, the monasteries still had their own jurisdiction and were administered by orders like the Cistercians and the Franciscans. The Cistercians in those early years of rule still followed the non-Roman ways, until emissaries from Rome were sent to break their old allegiance with the Culdee rules.

The monastic complex of Kilmacduagh also hosts Ireland's tallest round tower. It leans at a five degree angle. I will cover it in more depth in a separate chapter on round towers. The round tower is said to have been built in the tenth century but some local farmers believe it was built far earlier. On Holy Island in Lough Derg, a half brother of St Colman called St Caimin is said to have built another round tower, only a shadow of which remains. Colman visited Holy Island himself after an angel bade him to do so. Colman is said to have died in 630 and Caimin in 653. If Caimin built a tower then this adds weight to the round tower at Kilmacduagh having been built far earlier than the tenth century.

In the early centuries of Christianity, shamanic practices were undoubtedly widespread and interwoven into the fabric of the new religion. In relatively recent times, there have been similar peaceful examples of missionary activity when Christianity has been introduced into areas where nature-based religions prevailed. In such cases, the new religion has incorporated the ways of the past so as to work with the people, rather than against them. The missionaries embraced the old belief system and introduced a new element in order for Christianity to be accepted. It is not clear whether the Culdees sought active conversion to their religion. Certainly they seemed to stay small in number. Whatever their intent was, the Culdees created a bridge between the old Druid religion of their Celtic region with the new religion of Christianity

I would like to return to the life of St Senan, who I mentioned at the start of this chapter was associated with Scattery Island in the mouth of the Shannon. Like Holy Island, Scattery has seven churches and a round tower. Whether seven churches can still be seen is immaterial – in fact early travel accounts write of there being eleven churches there at one time (18). In mystical studies of the qualities of numbers, seven is the number for the perfected female in her myriad forms while the counterpart quality of the singular (represented by the round tower) is seen as the male seed or initial thought impulse. The numbers combine perfectly and suggest a place of balanced active energy. Churches are often built on sites that act like acupuncture points within a local energy system on the land. The round tower on Scattery Island was built first by St Senan but was unfinished until later according to local lore. (Again legend suggests that round towers were built earlier than the ninth or tenth century. It is doubtful they were built to stave off Viking invasion - for anyone could torch a tower and all the inhabitants would die without mercy.)

On Scattery, an angel is said to have guided Senan to a spot where he placed his staff like a root in the ground, and a spring issued forth. There he lived for the final twenty years of his life, having already built small oratories on many of the islets in the Shannon. Legends of Culdee saints depict them throwing their staffs across waters to choose where next to settle, or raising their staffs against a body of water in order that they would part and the party could cross with ease on the river or sea bed. As I said before, St Senan may even have been a pre-Christian figure who was Christianized. There is written evidence for this (18). He is first mentioned in the Betha (Irish Life) in association with one of his monasteries (more than likely Inis Scattery) when the Corcu Baiscinn clan were ruling (19). In an illuminating article the author argues the case that Senan was of Culdee ascetic persuasion. This vindicates my sense that he was a Culdee.

There is a bronze bell from the island in the British Museum. There was an ornamental shrine created to protect it and this bell shrine is in the National Museum in Dublin. There St Senan is traditionally depicted with an Egyptian style Tau cross staff, so common to the Culdees whose roots lay in Egypt. Senan is seen clutching what appears to be an Ark. At his feet lie two inter-twining dragons. This last feature leads us into the next chapter, where we shall see how Culdee saints such as Senan and Creich were associated with dragons, and explore why this was so.

1 Celt Druid and Culdee Isobel Hill Elder 1938 The Covenant Publishing Co Ltd London p 88

2 The Divine Matrix Gregg Braden 2007 Hay House Publishing ISBN 978-1-4019-0573-6 p63-66

3 The Neville Reader 2005 De Vorss and Company ISBN 9780875168111

4 Carmina Gadelica by Alexander Carmichael 1900

5 The Diocese of Killaloe Rev Philip Dwyer 1878 republished O'Brien Publications 1997 ISBN 0 9531 053 2 5 p2

6 History of Clare by Rev White republished 1997 O'Brien Book Publications 0-9531-053-1-7 p 4

7 The Diocese of Killaloe by Rev Philip Dwyer 1878 republished O'Brien Publications 1997 ISBN 0 9531 053 2 5 p 3

8 ibid p4

9 The Viking Serpent by Harald S Boehkle Trafford Publishing 2007   ISBN 141209755 – x p220

10 ibid p 219

11 ibid

12 the late Jack Smith of the Knights of St John in Torphicen told me this - he wrote a booklet on St Fechan, patron of Scottish parishes; a Culdee saint based in his village many hundreds of years beforehand.

13 First Templar Nation 2012 Freddy Silva ISBN 13-978-0-9852824-3-1 p 52, 169 pp

14 Book of the Dean of Lismore early sixteenth century East Perthshire

15 The Diocese of Killaloe Rev Philip Dwyer 1878 republished O'Brien Publications 1997 ISBN 0 9531 053 2 p 494

16 The Divine Blueprint 2012 Freddy Silva Invisible Temple ISBN 13: 978-0-9852824-4-p 204

17 Seed of Knowledge Stone of Plenty John Burke and Kaj Halberg ISBN1-57178-184-6 p10

18 The Stranger's gaze Travels in County Clare 1534-1950 1198 Clasp Press ed Brian O'Dalaigh ISBN 1 900545 08x p 142

19 Senan of Inis Cathaigh Gearoid O hAllmhurain Dal gCais Magazine no 4 p 53

Element Two

SPIRIT OF WOOD

Concluding remarks: On a purely physical level wood is present in trees, providing sustenance for life and creating a living landscape that creatures can thrive in. In fact much of life as we know it depends on the continued existence of forests.

On an emotional level the wood element holds the energy of the pioneering spirit, fuelled by forward thinking processes. I associate this aspect of the wood element with the Spirit of Early Christians, who often said Mass by ancient holy trees or in the Druid groves of oak and hazel. Wood stokes the fire, the next element in our cycle.

Element 3: Spirit of Primary Fire

FIERY DRAGON
I recoil as suddenly
your brazen eye stares out.
Dragon body coiling through
the tree of enchantment.
A fiery tendril
of wooden flames.
Then I breathe out
and see you
an old gnarled apple tree.
My protector and friend.

Element Three

Chapter 3 Dragon Myths

In this chapter I focus on the ancient primeval energies inherent in the land. These energies in the Earth can erupt to the surface where they then move along invisible lines of energy called ley lines, the lighter ones created within the electro-magnetic range. Known as leys or ley lines they can be wavy or straight. Here I concentrate on the dragon leys which are often referenced in a disguised form in myth.

The fire element belongs to the dragons that lay the primordial leys in the land. Without their fiery works, the earth would be devoid of that inner passion it needs to thrive. Dragon leys lie deep with the earth. They are intensely feminine in nature and at times are concealed within dragon myths. The dragon leys supported Ireland through its Golden Age of illumination and in its rich pre-Christian heritage. The Celtic saints often honoured the dragon leys and stories of them slaying dragons ought not to mislead. The monks would have been aware of the immense creative power within the land, and knew how to harness it for good. I will explore some relatively unknown dragon myths of the Burren, which serve as reference points to the earth energies. These dragon myths are bound up with the lives of the early saints who were akin to shamans too. I call this chapter "Dragon Myths" in honour of the feminine creative principle that lies deep within the land.

Many people sense a sacred atmosphere in the Burren, partly because the landscape is relatively unspoilt. There is more though that does not readily meet the eye about this region. It contains dragon leys that silently sustain it. I would purport in our current climate that the dragon leys badly need some loving attention from the human realm. The Earth benefits from loving thoughts from the human realm towards it. After all, human thoughts are a form of etheric energy. They do not simply dissipate but are part of the whole etheric envelope which we and the land contribute to, since the land too is sentient. This fact is known to this day by all indigenous cultures who revere the land not as a commodity to exploit for money but as a living sentient being whose health and very state of being depends on our attitude towards it.

Mythology plays an important role in landscape interpretation for me and many others. Sacred lore stems from human consciousness interacting with the powers and presences of the landscape, atmosphere and stars. Often such places are bound up with initiation. Temple makers seek out the spots where the influence of these forces interweave and are strong. (1)

Dragons in mythology represent the core energies of a place and their specific locations offer clues on how to read the land. In Britain, the dragon myths have survived fairly intact. In Ireland the concept of a dragon has not been so much to the fore, though remnants survive. For instance, I noted a newspaper article in Clare promoting the Shannon dragon or monster Caithach in a tourism concern. I thankfully knew that there was more to the dragon than a marketing ploy. Indeed, when I moved to Ireland I had scoured the excellent local history archives in Ennis, County Clare for stories of dragons, sensing there may be some. Dragons hold the most potent, almost primeval, forms of earth energies available to man's perceptions, and they shape the pathways to come. In Australian Aboriginal culture the lines the dragons make on their travels are called "song lines" upon which the Aborigines walk long, long distances, "toning" as they go.

Toning is an extremely powerful exercise to try out when alone in nature. The human voice box has an amazing range of vibrations, and you can use your voice as an instrument to commune with nature. Toning enables you to feel more keenly the life force or energy field that surrounds the land, as well as its innermost dragon forces. How is it done? It has to be done in a relaxed state. It is quite simple as all you have to do is relax, tune in to yourself, and then with that inner quiet feel the land around you. As you stay in that still space start to intuit what sounds to produce without over-thinking. Let the sounds come and almost immediately you can feel your energy field expand and your senses heighten. You may even feel yourself having a conversation with the inner heart of the land!

The Celtic chants sung by Druids and priestesses in ancient times were designed to facilitate an expansion of consciousness, so that they could pick up messages from the invisible realms. When I toned specific Celtic chants with others in a cave in Roslin Glen I knew that there were exceedingly important ley lines traversing our space. The chanting was led by Fiontullach, who is the head of the Ceili De order of Hermetics in Scotland. As I mentioned in the last chapter, Fiontullach is a discriminating teacher of the ancient Celtic bardic tradition. She possesses a great knowledge and can impart various levels of knowledge through story and chant. Very often I have found sacred chant in unity with nature to produce the most other-worldly results. In some instances unexplained phenomena, such as light rays, have been captured on camera. Other times bird sound could be heard that was not of this world. Sound when used correctly can certainly help connect us to the earth's cosmic energies. There is an inner earth vibration that animals seem to sense. We know that birds migrate according to the Earth's magnetic field that helps them to orientate their path. Some believe that birds fly along airborne paths that follow magnetic wavelengths. They probably can sense the miniscule changes in vibrations that the magnetic waves carry, and orientate themselves by this. Homing pigeons tend to recognise intersecting nodes of magnetic grid patterns and track these back to base! However it is the subtle and invisible energy lines in the earth that are more mysterious and one level more real. Tribal chiefs of Australian Aboriginal tribes believe that the whole Earth is connected through such lines that they name as "song lines". Once initiated into the art of using their psychic or spirit bodies, Aborigines travel vast distances along their magnetic song lines, connecting with other tribes on their continent.

Experiencing the effects of chanting on animals and birds helped me understand how the Aborigines engage with nature when they walk their song lines across the land. Their vocal offerings seem to nourish Gaia's nervous system. They are invoking the Dragon energy of the land to bless and protect them, and in return by recognizing the land they bless it. Recognition of the land actually feeds it energy. Once I travelled with a small group of Bedhouins in Jordan. I observed one man walk in a bee line to locate and interact with a large rock on such a subtle level that he was able to feed off the prana (energy) it emitted. He told me he did this at intervals in order to survive on very little food in the desert! He seemed to intuit a ley to walk on with an inborn knowledge that it led to what he needed at the time. These skills require a deep level of patience and acute powers of observation.

On the summer solstice of 2012, while on a tour with clients who followed the spiritual traditions of the ancient Inca, we chose to tone at one end, or pole, of a local dragon line in County Clare. This was specifically for a Dragon tour I had devised for them. Interestingly I had selected a Celtic ritual invoking the eight directions to use in conjunction with the toning, only to find their chosen Inca ritual was identical in nature! Despite the dull weather and subsequent lack of views of the Shannon estuary from Scattery Island that afternoon, we felt that familiar lift in our spirits as we stood inside the doorway of the round tower toning a simple chant with the expressed wish to bless the land. As I said, first I sense the space I am in and then engage in a free-flow style of chanting that opens me up as a conduit for the energies to pass through. I feel linked to the inner earth as my mind does not get in the way as it normally would! It felt special to be standing on an island in the Shannon on the Solstice of 2012. Interestingly the following year two missing stone heads were returned to the island as part of the Gathering festival. Likewise two stone heads were found in Holyrood Park, an ancient sanctuary in Edinburgh during the time I was taking people there to meditate on a significant ley line. A head symbolizes the main cornerstone in the metaphysical Reshel system I was studying at the time, and the synchronicity of a similar event occurring after we did a ceremony on Scattery Island is interesting to note. Whenever I lead these meditations we do not go with any human intent but ask that the Masters on the inner plane use our session for wherever spiritual light is needed.

When I studied acupuncture in relation to massage and sound healing I realised the great similarities that lie between my interest in Gaia (Earth as a sentient being) and our own human health. I often compare the land to the human body. Like the human body the Earth is sentient and contains blood vessels (rivers), neural pathways (dragon lines), meridians (ley lines) and chakra points (vortices of earth energies). To my pleasant surprise one day while out on a ramble near Gort I met a mild-mannered farmer who shared this same viewpoint: he had observed the land on his farm for many years and had obviously taken great care in tending to it. He talked with a quiet passion for the land, adding that it contains its own meridians in the same way that humans do. The planting on his land was exceptionally well thought out and proves how local knowledge of the earth meridians pays dividends in terms of good custodianship.

What exactly is this dragon energy within the context of earth energies? I believe that the dragon represents at one level the powerful ley lines that move within the land and sea beds, acting as part of the nervous system in our body, carrying subtle messages to our organs and muscles so we can function in harmony. Viewing the planet as a giant brain, the dragon lines can be likened to the neural pathways of white matter that carry messages across wider areas, connecting one part of the nervous system to another.

(By contrast, grey matter carries more local information.)

Ley lines by contrast serve as meridians (energy pathways with various functions) which carry the coded information between polarities on the land and even across the intervening seas. While leys are often straight the movement of underground water creates wavy leys that always twist. They too can be dowsed/divined. My own grandfather was a water diviner for his neighbourhood in County Clare. (Dowsing is often called divining in Ireland but I prefer to apply this term to water dowsing only.)

When water runs above ground it performs a special function too. Rivers are like the veins that hold and continually recycle the memory of the land. These veins transport the blood in our body and provide a structure for the blood flow. Rivers are the very life force that the land needs to draw upon in order to give itself its unique qualities. Similarly seas are a mass of water that are akin to the universal life force and are more like a giant fluid force of will power. Since leys move between countries they have to cross seas. Sailors and early monks would have been aware of the ley lines at sea and on land as they sailed or walked respectfully. Island towers act like important acupuncture points connecting various lands so that each land can communicate with the other. Drawing on the sea energy, the towers amplify the energies and attract dragon leys. No wonder dragons are associated with seas and lakes, for without these bodies of water nothing could be transmuted into action.

In summary the dragon energy or dragon spirit travels along sympathetic pathways that connect one place to another, allowing the energy of Mother Earth to flow better. They underlie a loose-knit network of ley lines that provide an etheric structure that feeds and harmonizes the Earth. Meanwhile, water channels replenish the spirit of the land by carrying vital information to receptors in the earth that renew the blood of the land. I am painting a picture here to help communicate the etheric processes at hand.

A dragon in mythology shapes the colour of the land. In early Christian times the monster was still recognized as a life force to contend with. The dragons once were feared, for man felt he had no control over it. He was at the mercy of nature and life was pretty precarious. On the other hand dragons were respected. According to a mystic Coleston Brown (2) residing in Ireland, the slaying or defeating of a dragon marks the setting of a power centre in the landscape. It does not mean the dragon is the enemy: it is a force to be harnessed. For me I feel that when the spear enters the earth it is in effect pouring in the life blood of the dragon. This blood carries codes from both the skies and the deep earth as the inner earth is aligned with cosmic energies. Anywhere that there is a church or folly dedicated to St Michael (such as Glastonbury Tor) the energies are high. The act of piercing the dragon acknowledges the presence of a ley line, or even multiple leys crossing, which are now anchored so they can be more effective.

I think the dragon lines have to be seen within a wider context of consciousness too. When Michael the Archangel speared the dragon it symbolized his commitment to protecting the whole of the Earth for these times. The act of Longinus spearing Christ on Golgotha is a deeply esoteric matter relating to ancient earth mysteries. In the Gospel stories Christ's wound spilled both blood and water onto the earth. In many ways Christ was embodying the dragon in this cosmic event. Mystics such as Ruldolf Steiner have shared deep insights into these mysteries and the event has significance far beyond that accorded to it by traditional Christian theology. Golgotha means "(place of) the skullpan of a head". In the Reshel, the mystical tradition I studied in relation to a global network of ley lines, the skull is interpreted as a deeply meaningful symbol. The name "Reshel" means "chief headstone of God". The skull denotes a place of great power when a landscape feature is associated with it. It usually becomes the control point for complex energetic systems.

In esoteric Christian terms, the Golgotha mystery signifies the creation of a new centre that was not bound to the location of Golgotha. As mystics such as Steiner testify, Christ's death was an event that freed all sentient beings on Earth to evolve along the path of co-creation. The act was for the world as a whole, for cosmic forces flowed in to Earth from the wider cosmos and a totally new vibration entered the Earth. Christ's dramatic "death" marks the point in time when humans could take a step forward in responsibilities and start to co-create life on Earth, rather than relying on unknown forces of destiny or nature alone. The act renewed the land and heralded a new paradigm that mankind has yet to fully recognize. Remember, the land and humanity are inextricably linked beyond the physical levels.

Long after the Christ event, it is arguably only now that mankind has started to shake off his fear of the dragon; his fear of unknown forces of nature. His fear of "female" wild energies also can be likened to the subconscious. As man learns to work with and even transform the subconscious that often holds his fears, the cultural view of nature alters simultaneously, and in the eleventh hour man can still become the custodian of the Earth, rather than

Nature's rapist.

This introduces a more psychological interpretation of the dragon energy as a wild untamed force of nature, akin to the subconscious on a human mental level. Please be patient with this long preamble as it serves a necessary purpose in painting a picture. The earlier spiritual viewpoint for the Celts was that nature was a powerful force to be reckoned with and that man had little control over it. They wove its power into their stories using different creatures to ascribe its varying qualities. The magic of the Druids was consulted in order to live with the dragon energy in relative harmony. After the advent of the Christ the nature of the dragon energy shifted as did everything else. Rather than fearing it man could now become more conscious of the dragon energy and harness it for good purposes.

It was as if the Pagan faith was misaligned with the incoming consciousness in the late Iron Age, and without understanding or focussing on the new Christ energy, their way of life had to wane. The dragon no longer held sway over men - and there was a necessary shift in consciousness in order that eventually man could become a co-creator like Jesus who embodied the Christ energy. The Christ energy is only now after two thousand years rooting itself, with people starting to understand that religion aside, the Christ energy has the power to transform lives, and exponentially develop human wisdom and love.

As noted above, when Michael the Archangel speared the dragon it symbolized his commitment to protecting the whole of the Earth. Legends of the Culdees are often associated with taming or piercing/killing dragons in the same way that Archangel Michael did, for whilst this archangel is chiefly responsible for assisting the Earth's evolutionary path, human agents have also played a vital role in the drama. The Culdees were one such specialist group who clung to pockets of the UK and Ireland, helping ground this angelic mission. The Culdees were a good example of how to embrace the potential for change, using their spiritual connections achieved through meditation and prayer wisely for the good of all. They became splendid examples of custodianship as they worked with the earth rather than in fearful abjection to it. They were healers with a heritage rich in knowledge of the archangels, who also intimately embraced knowledge of the devic kingdoms/lower heavens.

Returning to the dragon myths now, in west Clare lies the aforementioned small island of Scattery, in the mouth of the river Shannon. One legend has it that Michael the Archangel transported St Senan on a flagstone to the island where Senan came face to face with a dragon called Catach. A battle ensued and Catach lost to Senan. The slain dragon was thrown into Doo Lough, a lake below the holy hill of Slieve Callan on the mainland. Places of power are often underlain by bodies of water and here is no exception. As receptor of the dragon energy, the lake could well be recycling its energies to this day, and is more than likely one of the invisible forces that influence the rich musical and oral traditions in West Clare, for music and stories deftly embody the invisible realms.

In Liscannor Bay, on the edge of the thin dunes close to the seaside town of Lahinch, lies the old ruined church of our old friend St Creich. The siting of the church has a bearing on the following myth: St MacCreehy banished a dragon to the sea here. The same myth talks of a corpse-eating eel that he killed. The church used to bear a few carvings of the dragon, including one of him holding a long bone in his jaws. Sites with serpents or dragons carved on them can denote a passing of a ley line. All I could find in St McCreehy's church was an worn old carving over a lintel of a cat-like beast with long pointed ears, large eyes and huge jaws with teeth showing.(3) There is a similar carving to be seen on Scattery Island where St Creich used to reside too. Cats are another common emblem of the rampant earth energies that course through the land. St MacCreehy, alias St Creich, also is said to have slain a phantom badger of immense proportions at Rath Blathmaic inland. (4) St Creich disposed of the "broc sidhe", or fairy badger, by dumping the body in beautiful Lough Ra nearby. Pronounced "Ra" the name echoes that of the Egyptian solar deity! It may be that chasing and overthrowing the dragon, or suchlike beast, symbolises diverting or eliminating electro-magnetic energies that are detrimental to man. Another possibility is that if the dragon is pierced, then the energy is anchored so a church or temple can be built in safety. The phantom badger still rises every seven years if you are (un)lucky enough to encounter it!

Returning to Kilmacreehy (meaning Church of son of Creehy), there is another legend that correlates well with the immediate locale. According to local coldwater divers I talked with once, there is a shelf out to sea in Liscannor Bay that has forests and bogs intact. There are even arches and ridges to dive through. Local legend says there is a lost village called Kilstefan lying beyond the shore, and variations of the myth tell of a palace city with golden domes upon its roofs. In around 799-802 an earthquake is said to have split some land into three islands off the coast between Kilmacreehy and Scattery Island, and drowned tens of scores of men, along with the church of Kil Stefan. Mutton Island where Senan had prayed was split into three parts. While St MacCreehy lived at least two hundred years earlier, in folk memory the earthquake event may have been twinned with the work of the dragon(5). Folklore has placed this dragon in the sea, never to return again. In 1750 John Windele wrote a popular novel that mentioned dragon temples located at Scattery on the Shannon, the nearby promontory of Loop Head on the mainland and Inismaan (the middle of the three Aran Isles nearby). What inspired him to describe the general area in such a manner?

I want to continue with the theme of the human subconscious in relation to the dragon energy. As I said earlier, in ancient times the wild untamed forces of nature were akin to what modern psychology calls the subconscious. Man feared this force because he felt he had no control over it. In as much the way he could not foresee an earthquake arising.... he had little control over his subconscious. The vast power of nature was woven into story forms, using different creatures and events to personify its varying qualities. If myths mirror reality in the past we learn that it was necessary for people to consult with seers in order to live in harmony with this unforeseen dragon-like energy. Almost as a form of insurance for a fairly precarious life, various myths show how the true worth of the dragon was acknowledged and even appeased from time to time. As time progressed the forces of nature were tamed more and the dragon stories receded too. We entered a more linear and less cyclical pattern of thinking, in which man naturally distanced himself more from his subconscious and myths became folk tales with lesser depth to them.

Today there is a parallel process that we all partake in to some degree or other, which is open to each of us when we dream. There the subconscious resides with no limits. Some years ago I noticed that the physical act of journeying strengthens my own subconscious. It is as if my intuitive juices flow more when I am on the move rather than when I remain on one spot. Perhaps since I am in relatively unknown territory my richer subconscious life feeds me various clues how to navigate. More poignantly I find that dreaming allows me to process the energy of the land I am passing through at a subconscious level, so that my soul receives the messages it requires for healthy growth. I genuinely feel that through my dream life I am able to receive the subtle energies of the Earth as well as cosmos.

Element Three

There is a darker side to all this progress, and it is a side with which many may associate more than the earlier dragon interpretations I have given. Apart from likening dragons to ley lines, or nature at its wildest, or forces of the unknown subconscious, since industrialization a new dynamic gained popularity, and is only now waning in those parts of the world which are post-industrial: dragons were likened to dark forces associated with the female. It was expedient to do so. The male quality was perceived as the acceptable, reasoning voice, while the female became this voice to be subdued. In the process of subduing her qualities, the female energies started to be equated with illogic, and even lunacy. This was not a balanced picture and could not last. The euphemistic tale of St Patrick banishing the snakes alias dragons from Ireland carries with it a cautionary note. There is a danger that ignoring a quality makes it rear its head in an exaggerated condition. Her processes were cyclical and process-oriented whilst His were linear and goal-oriented. Nature suffers when the female energy is not respected.

Sadly as the true worth of the female energies went into long decline, the male patriarchal church and society came into being, a story we are all familiar with. Having nowhere to place this female – associative energy, the male, patriarchal Christian church emerged victorious and yet imbalanced. It is around this time that stories of slaying dragons emerged. It really depends on what level you choose to interpret the dragon! Although the dragon disappeared in all but the most tolerant corners of our reality, I would argue that the forces of the less seen, more unknown realms are returning in both the arts and the sciences. I personally feel that the arts and sciences are drawing closer again, as they take different routes to pursue their similar goals in seeking truth.

Of course the picture is not so black and white. I am painting a general picture and there have always been exceptions to the rule. Certainly the early Celtic saints of the Burren and Aran Isles appear to have been in touch with their feminine sides. In addition, they followed the dragon leys in siting their small cell churches. In both Scotland and Ireland there existed Culdee monks who possessed skills in geomancy (the art of siting buildings to encourage wellbeing and even good fortune). St Brendan of Birr who passed his skills on to both Columba and Brendan the Navigator (of Clonfert), Ciaran of Clonmacnoise, Aiden of Lindisfarne, Senan of the Shannon estuary, and Patrick were but a few whose names we know. On

64

Scattery Island an angel is said to have guided Senan to a specific spot where he placed his staff like a root in the ground. At this spot a spring issued forth. This to me denotes a ley is updating the local system. When these early saints threw their staffs across bodies of water to select a site upon which to settle, or when they parted the waters with their staff in order to cross over, or when they struck the land with their staff and a spring appeared, they were in effect tuning into the leys of the land. Rooted in the knowledge of the leys (as depicted by the dragons below his feet), Senan and others possessed geomantic skills like their predecessors. Whilst Senan was born too late to know Columba or Patrick, he followed on in their tradition and cemented their works. The round tower behaves like an acupuncture point in the land. It heralds a new energy complex that is supported by the requisite well/spring nearby. Round towers will be covered extensively in a later chapter.

Dragons and serpents are interchangeable symbols in mythology. St. MacCreehy whilst on a "diplomatic mission" visited an early church at Corcomroe. The story goes that an army of invaders from Connaught to the north chased a big serpent (synonymous with a dragon) up from Corcomroe as far as a massive cairn on the banks of the river Daelach in the townland of Daelach outside Ennistymon. There they slew the dragon and buried him inside the cairn (6). When I approached this cairn known as Cairn Connachtugh, I felt a veritable pulse of energy emanating from quite a distance away. I could understand then how suitable the cairn was to bury a dragon! Daelach was one of Ireland's earliest inhabitants and he too is said to be buried inside this cairn. As a brave chieftain, Daelach might have been comfortable to share his last resting place with a dragon! He had two Fir Bolg brothers: Irghus who is buried at Caherdooneerish stone fort near Black Head in the Burren, and Beara, who lived at Finnavara on the peninsula off the Burren a little further north. It was after the dragon energy was somewhat suppressed that the Cistercian monks moved into Corcomroe. Close to Corcomroe lies Oughtmama in a remote valley, where there were in all seven churches. No doubt the community at Oughtmama had lived in harmony with the dragon. I suspect that the divine feminine was acknowledged and integrated into the daily lives of the monks during this time. Now we will visit some superhuman heroes in the region, who seemed to embody the dragon energies.

1 Coleston Brown Secrets of a Fairy Landscape Illustrations Jessie Skillen 2012 Green Fire ISBN 978-0-9865912208 P33
2 ibid 59
3 Folklore of Clare TJ Westropp 2003 Clasp Press p27
4 ibid p27
5 ibid p3
6 ibid p100

SPIRIT OF PRIMARY FIRE

Concluding remarks: The fire element belongs to the dragons, that lay the primordial leys in the land. Without their fiery works the earth would be devoid of that inner passion it needs to thrive. Some relatively unknown local myths focus on early Christians slaying or chasing dragons. More than likely they "chased" the dragons along the Dragon leys, which are deeply embedded ley-lines in the land. The dragon leys supported Ireland in both its Golden Age of illumination and in its rich pre-Christian heritage. That same dragon energy coloured the myths of our folk heroes in the following chapter.

Spirit of Fire; Secondary Fire

Goddess of Future Myths
Who dreamt you into being
here where the vesica appears?
Crushing all disbelief
Your location
is exhilarating
Perfect accompaniment
To the one.

Element Three

Chapter 4 Fiery Heroes

This chapter looks at some interesting local myths that bear no direct relation to dragons, but are infused with that heroic spirit so often associated with inner fire. The myths indicate that people once were aware of the potent dragon energies and the realms that they dwelt in. Our mythical heroes invoked the co-operation of the Sidhe in our next chapter too.

The raw untamed nature of the dragon energy surfaces in various god-like figures in the mythologies of Ireland and elsewhere. This period of gods roaming the Earth and skies eventually subsided, and a new paradigm entered, when super-human heroes took those god-like qualities on board and owned them for themselves. There was no longer an external battle taking place between the various gods, but a more measured battle taking place, where humans were fallible as well as super-heroic, and some degree of internal battle crept in too. Nowhere perhaps does this ring truer than in the story we shall look at later of Diarmuid and Grainne, who were opposed by Grainne's husband Finn McCool (aka Fionn Mac Cumhaill), a mighty Milesian warrior.

It is useful to ask who these Milesians were. In some versions of the McCool saga they are said to be of the Scotti tribe. Many thought, until recently when academic opinion started to change, that the Scotti lived in the north of Ireland for some period preceding the fifth century AD. Then they expanded their territory into Atlantic Scotland. St Columba was of the Dal Riada sept of the Scotti tribe in Donegal, and Scotland apparently gained its name from these settlers. Another more metaphysical version of Scottish history has it that the origin of Scotland derives from a Milesian princess named Scotia, who sailed from Egypt through the Mediterranean. Scotia is supposed to have lived in the Tara temple complex. Her father was a pharaoh in Egypt and her husband a Scythian warrior. Her child Gaedel Glas fashioned the Gaelic language from seventy two languages (72 = 6 x 12 and is a cosmic number). The Scotti derived their name from Scotia/Scota in this version of their origins.(1)

Maia Nartoomid wrote of Scota's journeys in her own vast body of channelled material, printed in various issues of Temple Doors in the 90s (2).

The princess is said to have stopped by the Canary Islands. When visiting the small island of El Hiero I did suddenly come across a giant statue of a sheela-na-gig created by a local potter who placed it in her rambling garden. I enquired who it was and was told it was Tara the earth goddess of the island! I then told the local people how I had just come from Tara in Ireland and how that image of fecundity was often inscribed over the doorways of medieval churches. They were surprised to hear this and had not heard of Tara the ancient centre in County Meath in Ireland. The Milesians overthrew the earlier De Danaan inhabitants at the Battle of Tailte in County Meath.

It is difficult to pinpoint dates for the various incursions of foreign invaders into Ireland, but the De Danaan descended from the goddess Danu and may well have lived with the earlier Fir Bolg from the start. According to mythology, after the Battle of Tailte some time around 2000 BC, the Milesian judge gave the De Danaan all in the underworld to rule, while his own people ruled all that which was above the earth. (Some say that the De Danaan never went wholly underground and that there are those living among the present day Irish who are "fey", as they are of Danaanite fairy blood.) This division of Ireland into over-ground and underground races reminds me of the way the rivers dip under and over the land around Gort on the eastern side of the Burren. Small wonder that this was one of the last strongholds for Celtic legends and stories! It is these stories that local aristocrats such as WB Yeats and Lady Gregory sought to collect at the start of the twentieth century. It would make an interesting project to search them for older references to inner earth dwellers and such like.

In later centuries the "Celts" arrived. In Britain, there were two waves of Celts that swept west. The first wave came from central Europe and beyond in around 400BC. In Ireland we know that a separate wave of Celts came in from north Africa and Spain as evidenced by the similarities in language, singing styles and even fishing vessels between north Africa and Ireland. (The work of film maker and researcher Bob Quin provides notable references.)

More than likely the original location of all Celts was east of the Altai Mountains in Siberia, where rock art similar to that depicted at the height of the Celtic culture can be seen. The dragon was frequently depicted in Celtic art of course- even up to the time when holy manuscripts were painstakingly designed. The dragons in the elaborate knot work of missals such as the Book of Kells were finely executed and prolific. This short foray into Celtic history hopefully creates some context to the tales of heroes that are related in this chapter.

Finn McCool was chasing his wife and her lover across Ireland. He chased them from their hiding place on the shores of Lough Graney (Graney means "Sun") in east Clare, on past Inchiquin Hill in the Burren and then to Seefin near Black Head. Often known as "Diarmid and Grainne's beds", there are many portal tombs that lace their chase. The dolmens near Doolin on the west coast are associated with the final stages of the race to escape his wrath. Diarmid heaped seaweed onto a dolmen under which they were sheltering, in a bid to prevent Finn finding them. Finn possessed a magical thumb which whenever he licked it would reveal a picture of where his target lovers were. When Finn licked his CCTV thumb and saw nothing but seaweed all over a clump of rocks, he wrongly surmised the hapless lovers had drowned in the Atlantic. He ceased pursuing them. Clever Diarmid had outwitted Finn, who also lost his favourite hound in the chase. The hound is buried under a cairn in his name on Black Head.

In this period when Finn appears, there is a charming lesser known local legend that takes place in the heart of the Burren. While Finn and his warriors were camping on the Howth peninsula outside of Dublin there lived unbeknown to them a member of the Tuath de Danaan, who having three arms and only one leg must surely have been one of the most extraordinary people that ever lived on Earth! He lived in the townland of Teeskagh in the Burren, close to a mountain named after his magical cow Glas Ghoibhneach. His own name was Lon Mac Loimhtha and he was widely known as Lon the Smith, for he was the first person to have made edged weapons in Ireland. It is said he lived even before the time that there was steel or iron implements- when bronze, flint and stone were used. So he spanned the entire De Danaan period by all accounts.

Sliabh na Glasha (pronounced Slievenaglasha) is a place where time and space collide splendidly. Lon lived and worked in an elusive cave in a field called Garraidh na Cartan. The rock upon which the cave was hewn was known as the "Forge of Lon, Son of Liomtha", and cinders and dust lined the floor of his humble home. He used his third arm as an anvil to turn the iron on. This arm grew from the centre of his chest. When he had to travel, he used his solitary leg as a pedestal from which he could bound across hills and valleys at a great pace!

Lon had seven sons who tended his cow one day a week by turn. Every night they would turn the cow round to face her bed, and she would sleep on this same spot. To this day no blade of grass grows there on the Leaba na Glaise (tr:Cow's Bed). Lon had stolen the cow from Spain (maybe from the Milesians who now were invading?) and he and the cow had travelled far and wide in Ireland before settling on this fertile mountain. There was no vessel that this cow could not fill with her own abundant milk - until one day with Lon's consent a local woman bought a disguised sieve to milk her with. This time the milk passed through the bottom of the vessel, and as it overflowed it divided into seven rivulets called the Seven Streams of the Overflowing (Teescach, or Teeskagh). The copious milk turned into streams of pure water which to this day form cascades over the cliff in winter.

Remember that the De Danaan had been banished to live with the Sidhe (fairies) and were branded as wizards and witches, secreted in caves and underground chambers. Lon alone seemed to defy the order and travelled above ground periodically. Hearing of the fame of Finn MacCool, Lon set out to meet him. In a few hops he reached the Howth peninsula where he boldly announced his arrival as "Lon the Smith of Letha" adding as his profession a smith. He lay a "gesa", an obligatory challenge: he had to be overtaken on his return journey to his forge. He then took to his heel and returned in his usual bounds. However, one of Finn's warriors, Caoilte, was so swift that he arrived there ahead of Lon! Lon soon caught up with him and welcomed him into his home, announcing that the gesa had been a mere ruse to entice the warriors over, so he could personally make them swords and other edged weapons of sure destruction! At the end of three days Finn and seven of his warriors joined Coilte, and Lon made them eight swords all tempered and steeled. The swords were so strong the warriors Goll and Genan broke the smith's anvil with their swords when they struck it. Then Finn and his warriors went to the summit at Ceann Slieve, where members of the Tuatha De Danaan had stationed themselves to guard all principal causeways leading to the green and beautiful hill in Teeskagh. Finn and his seven men attacked the De Danaanites with the same swords fashioned by Lon, cutting them into pieces. They left the bones of the De Danaanites on the summit where they dug them out daily to prevent them from resting! No one knows what happened to Lon, though rumour has it that his cow was stolen by an Ulster man shortly afterwards, forcing him to make a living from his smith craft alone.

This tale is very interesting as the number seven is repeated in it several times. From a metaphysical point of view, the number Seven represents the divine feminine aspect of creation, in its most perfect form. Seven sons protect the eternal source of bounty and fertility: the cow. She is the sacred animal associated in myth with the Milky Way in the sky, where the Pleiades star cluster resides. In many myths, we have seven women who represent the Pleiades. However there are seven sons, not seven daughters, in our myth here. When sexes switch over it usually denotes a higher level of initiation is taking place and a higher system of energy is being installed. In ancient Hebrew gematria (calculated by assigning numbers, or qualities, to each letter of a word in order to understand its inner meaning), the sacred number 7 requires an additional 1 in order for balanced and strong energy to manifest. We have this same system described with Finn and his warriors, and Lon and his protectors. It makes for a couplet of 7+1s, creating polarity that is essential for energies to manifest. The eight swords are fashioned and they strike the anvil of creation. This executive strike heralds a change in consciousness. Like a Greek tragedy Lon has been instrumental in orchestrating the takeover of power as if he sees a divine progression he cannot halt. This is how the shift in consciousness is told.

On a more normal level of interpretation the cow of plenty has yielded to the warrior of might - the nature-rich economy now has changed to a more mistrustful society that the small petty chiefdoms of Celtic society eventually adopted. Internal power struggles and boundary issues dominated until the brief arrival of the Golden Age of Celtic monks, with their collective message of peace and humility. Dragons still figured in stories of the early monks though often they are described as snakes (and snakes were absent or extremely rare in Ireland!). St Patrick banishing the snake is viewed by some as an allegory for the subconscious aspect of man yielding to the domain that is under his conscious control. On a deeper level, I see it that the female forces that are known to assist, support and create life from the eternal silence (represented by the sacred cow too) are subtly denigrated to the "evil shadows".

I would argue that in the Burren this shift toward the masculine never really took root, and I hear of local priests to this day who honour the beauty of nature and all things feminine, a vital part of the essential Divine presence. In short, the landscape of the Burren is divinely feminine.

1.The Book of the Taking of Ireland part 2 R A Steward translator 1939 (Irish Text Society) Educational Company for Ireland
2. e.g. Temple Doors Volume 98 The Grail Through Amega p 57 Maia Nartoomid
http://www.spiritstoreonline.com/publications.html

SPIRIT OF SECONDARY FIRE

Concluding remarks: The "Spirit of Heroes" of local myths indicates that people once were aware of both the potent dragon energies and the fairy realms. Fire as an element supports the Earth element, wherein the Sidhe or fairy energies reside.

Element 4: The Spirit of Earth

SUN-DAPPLED SIDHE RATH
Sylvan navel
There is nowhere I would rather be
than among the Sidhe
enclosed by hazel grove
encircled by moss.
Elementals in the tinkling of leaves
Addressing the shadows scattered
On an old, holy ground.

Element Four

Chapter 5 The Sidhe

Fire as an element supports the Earth. As it burns it yields ashes that are beneficial to the soil, releasing rich minerals which feed the earth. Over long stretches of time volcanoes have left rich soils in their wake, resplendent with minerals that are of value to our health. In the cycle of this book the etheric energies concern us more. The fiery dragon lines nourish the fairy kingdom, helping to create a healthy number of fairies or nature spirits who support nature's growth.

There are various names in various cultures for the nature spirits who have many subdivisions. In Ireland the generic name for these spirits is the Sidhe (pronounced "shee"), and often where Christians "colonised" an area, place-names reflected the old pantheon of nature gods and spirits which were renamed after saint associations. In our modern era the qualities of the fairies and other spirits are often overlooked. They hold the space for stellar energies to reside within the earth. This chapter on the Spirit of Sidhe honours them and talks of specific areas and events in the Burren that reflect their magic.

There is a symbiotic relationship between the Sidhe and the earth's geomantic energy. In other words the deep dragon lines co-exist with the Sidhe or fairies that dwell in and around the earth. Earth lives on because of all the ongoing work of its numerous nature spirits or devas.

In the olden days stories spoke of the Sidhe (pronounced "shee" meaning fairies) and other such things in a way that engaged the listener from the heart, stirring their imagination to other imaginary realms. A good story has the power to affect the listener at a subtle level. If you go, for instance, to the townland of Teeskagh and stand above the seven streams that flow there, you may be stirred to imagine that the water represents the Seven Sister planets in the Plaeides, and that there are energies pouring down from the Milky Way in the sky, connecting with Mother Earth. The Glas cow with her ever-flowing milk could well be a euphemism for this galaxy, where the Earth, as a star, in turn was born. There is something primeval about the plateau that cannot be adequately expressed in words. The whole area has a regenerating aspect to it. Sensing these qualities requires an openness to the possibility that such qualities exist in the landscape. The land then can act as the initiator into a heightened sense of awareness. Walking a landscape sensitively will awaken sensations in those seeking to understand the land, from an energetic point of view. What is vital to comprehend is that our awakening to the land is really reflecting the level of awakening to oneself. Our response to the Earth's qualities reflects to the limits of what we are capable of sensing.

Straddling the world of Christianity and the world of Paganism lies a zone of twilight beliefs that focus on the fairy energies. Until very recently the belief in the Sidhe in Ireland was very strong, but during the country's recent and rapid transition to a more urban culture, much of the rural identity has withered. For many the Sidhe is becoming a quaint myth. Yet it is still lurking in the shadows, and was certainly embraced by those who introduced Christianity to Ireland. Like so many areas of the world where that religion was exported, it was paramount to incorporate the folk beliefs and native religions into an adapted form of Christianity. Long before there was a definitive Church of Rome, the earlier forms of Christian faith (such as the Culdees) may well have contained a deep appreciation and strong respect for the elements of nature. It is these elements with which the Sidhe are intertwined.

On old OS maps there are many Gaelic place names for the streams and hills that are named after spirits whom humans have connected with the landscape features. In the days before urbanisation the people understood the qualities of local natural features, and sensed when the spirits (often of deceased humans), or the fairies/elementals, dwelt in them. The fairies to this day lend a distinct quality to a place. It was wise to mediate between their world and that of the mundane human one with some form of small ritual or prayer. This was a mark of respect for those who are not of our kind. When wells and other places were being renamed after Christian saints, there was but a thin veneer covering the tacit acceptance of another dimension among the Celtic races. The Irish are known to think and respond in a slightly less linear way than that of their European neighbours. Perhaps the De Danaan blood does indeed live on in them as some still maintain! They certainly attached great belief in the wells and their fairy associations.Fundamentally everything is made of energy, and the different qualities that the energies possess go at various times and places by the names of spirits. Fairies as we know them traditionally are in essence elementals or nature spirits. They inhabit nature and are also known as nature beings. Fairy stories relate the human perception of the fairies' varying qualities. Each fairy exhibits personality traits that relate to something in the natural world with which they are connected.

Many people perceive the Burren to be a major fairy place in Ireland. The fairy energies are almost tangible there. In the Burren there are many "green roads" where one can walk without disturbance from motor cars. These are ideal routes upon which to walk and feel the fairy surrounds. In the Burren there have been instances when walking its green roads that I have sensed the air change, and an all too familiar quality creep in. There is a sense of having entered some sacred space. Some describe it as a place where the air becomes thin. As I am sure many of you have experienced when walking in nature, at times a discernible change of mood can come from the surroundings rather than from deep within you. This can be caused by some wordless communication from the fairy realms that I perceive as a sudden sense of other-worldliness. I sometimes dowse with a pendulum to confirm that there is a distinct change in quality in the environment. In a later chapter I will discuss this in more detail. I have dowsed for many years and find that in some specific issues relating to the land connections I can be very accurate.

Fairy energies can be very subtle. Once when I was walking up the slopes of Slieve Elva I was drawn towards a small hawthorn grove growing in isolation among the rocks. I left the track, and as I near the spot I noticed two main trees in the centre, standing quite close to one another. Something compelled me to take out my camera and take some pictures. Later when I downloaded the pictures, I noticed one of the photos was showing a vortex of energy with everything spinning, creating an oval gap in the centre where the trees stood. I remembered that when I took the photo I was standing between these trees and sensing some kind of portal. I do not recall moving the camera, and even if I had done so, the resultant photo sums up the quality of my experience standing there.

Often it is the way of the elementals to respond to a wave of high energy frequencies. When they adjust to our more noble feelings it automatically affects the vibrational field around us. These vibrational energies consist of wavelengths that are longer than the normal light wavelengths of colour and light. Digital camera technology is far more sensitive to wavelength frequencies than the old fashioned SLR cameras were. Since it can detect minor changes in electrical energy fields, any atmospheric vibrations can show up. This interplay between the operator and the machine is a field that still can be explored more I feel. I find it exciting that light orbs are showing up far more on digital photographs - there is a growing array of variety in these orbs too. I have seen orbs in old tree trunks, in caves and both within and without sacred buildings. Sometimes I see them through the camera but not when the image is downloaded and vice versa. It fascinates me that something that cannot be seen with the naked eye is apparent to the camera mechanism used. Sometimes people have asked professional photographers to verify that what has appeared on the photo is indeed inexplicable. Perhaps the elementals are accepting the energy and transforming it into a denser form that we can see, at least when using digital photography. Quantum physics has long ascertained that human perception and emotions can alter outcomes: it appears that when we appreciate something in nature we alter our vibrational field, as verified in digital photography.

Elementals or nature beings support life processes, and fairies in the traditional sense are but one branch of this support. Fairy energies can also describe deeper earth mysteries and the occult - so the term "fairy" can be misleading. There are very sacred levels of Sidhe deep within the earth in addition to the light energies of the fairies that are attached to the various elements we already looked at. Also there are fairy energies who work with distant cosmic events. The elementals nourish the earth and the deeper elementals are harder to contact than angels. They can ally themselves with the developing earth grids mentioned in a later chapter, and help draw in cosmic energies.

A lot depends on our own frame of mind and degree of faith in them as to whether we see fairies or not. Once in the not so distant past, the notion that people saw fairies implied that they were a little unhinged mentally. Nowadays in more enlightened areas of the world it is becoming acceptable that people see things according to their state of mind, without judgement on whether it is true or not. Whether or not one believes in fairies really does depend on one's sense of reality. Entities emanating from the fairy realm were observed in a more widespread manner when people as a nation believed in them. I would propound that the fairies are still all around us - it is just that we have blocked out to a large extent the possibility of seeing them. Children who are innocent still see them. I once encountered a couple of fairies when I was young, and their conversation and the love they shared has remained with me forever.

I believe we see what we can accept and blot out the rest. It reminds me of the story of the South American Indians not seeing the invading Spanish ships on the horizon. They had no way of placing the image within a context, so their minds haplessly ignored what was there in front of them! Similarly, nature spirits or elementals appear in different guises, for they are really energies, or life forces, that support and sustain nature. Since we are for the most part still unused to seeing life in its etheric form we might not register it if we saw an etheric phenomenon... we might easily blot it out at the subconscious level. I know I used to see lights dancing in front of me as I walked through my local Roslin Glen - but if I stopped to look squarely at them they would surely disappear again. I could only perceive the lights out of the corner of my eye. Many people have described their experiences to me of communicating in a non-verbal way with the elementals in Roslin Glen, and I created a book of photos and poems to honour this most magical glen that I had the good fortune to live beside for some years. (1)

In rural Ireland, there still is a widespread belief in fairy rings which look like circular elevated ridges of grass in a field. People believed that fairies inhabited these rings, The smaller ones can be where the grass is paler in a ring. These are flatter and without any stone ridges on the circumference. It is said the rings were made by the fairies dancing on the spot, and no farmer will plough inside them to this day in many parts of Ireland. The larger rings seem to have been small fortified domestic settlements abandoned from a bygone era. The spirits of the past still linger in such places and so have become known as fairies. Beautiful hawthorns, blackthorns, ash and oak that grow in such rings become havens for the Sidhe or nature spirits to inhabit. Thus the dilapidated forts of the Iron Age seem to possess both discarnate and nature spirits.

Often nature will shape itself into a form that mirrors the energy of the spirit inhabiting the natural object, whether it is plant or rock or tree or river. The gypsies used to revere certain trees and other life forms when the spirit emerged in them in this fashion. Cloud formations too can appear in various forms that reveal an inner energy to the perceiver. There is usually an energetic exchange involved that leaves the observer changed in some way.

I recall working with a film-maker in Roslin Glen some years ago. We were making a film on the earth energies and ley lines of Roslin Glen and Rosslyn Chapel; a film regrettably unpublished, due to lack of funding at that time. He experienced many lights on his film footage that as a professional he could not explain. He even took photographs of his footage to prove they were there. Ironically when he tried to email them to me the file would not open. Somehow I felt these entities are there for the moment and not to be captured in linear time. Likewise when he started to film shots of me in the glen, several blue tits appeared and flew in vertical spirals around his tripod, to the point where he had to give up attempting to film the beauty of nature. He then just stared in amazement at the sight of the birds' frenetic spiralling. He encountered many extraordinary phenomena with nature that he had never witnessed before, more than likely due to his intense exposure to the very energetic spiritual content I had written for the film. The constant focus on esoteric knowledge had gradually raised his vibrations, as he considered the subtle energies I was discussing. When we focus on other realities, our own mental frequencies alter, and we leave behind the linear dimension that we are programmed to dwell in. Form does follow thought. It is a universal law.

Another time, I was collating files from my computer with an architect who had kindly offered to hand-draw many pictures of the Green Men carvings in Rosslyn Chapel. I clicked on the document folder to find the files when unexpectedly a file from another folder started to print itself, even though the folder was closed! As it emerged from the printer against a backdrop of mutterings about what on earth was going on, I grinned. A full A4 size photograph of the rock formation known as Pan was delivered into the office. I said "Pan likes what we are doing and has come to say hello!" and an ashen-faced architect said "Rose (his wife) must never know about this! She would be seriously worried about me." I have met many who have such experiences, which they refuse to talk openly about afterwards. I let this one go but observed the typical dynamic at play.

We are far more likely to have unusual experiences if we possess an open mind. It can raise our vibrations to see beyond the denser reality that linear thinking supports. In Ireland, there is a propensity towards cyclical thinking, which typically lifts us out of the commonplace. However this talent appears to be mainly expressed in the arts. It has not as yet been extended to a collective view of nature. If applied to the natural world and the subtle dimensions within, our view of nature would inevitably shift from one as consumers to a more holistic view as being an intrinsic component of nature. Perceptions of reality might shift in a more conscious mode towards what is currently archived in folklore sections of museums and libraries.

There are elementals attached to each of the four main elements (earth, fire, air and water) though there is also a fifth element that represents the less tangible yet unifying quality of ether. The humid air is omnipresent in Ireland and the dominant element of water is at the core of the Irish psyche. To a seer, nature spirits often appear in the guise of soft or bright colours like a fairy mist, all floating in the air. Old folktales abound of lights being seen in hills or in the bog lands. Today people catch sight of them in clearings in the woods, where nature returns to work her magic. Boggy places that are too small for the bulldozers to ruin also can impart a sense of other-worldliness. These places thankfully retain a charm value in our spirit-lacking society. It is quite relaxing to walk through a wetland. There is a sense of nature being supported and left unadulterated. Their survival is essential. Let the fairy energy congregate and grow!

There is a deeper Sidhe energy too that is connected with the inner earth as well as with the skies. Esotericists regard these deeper fairy energies as bridges between the stars and the Earth. It is much rarer for humans to experience these deeper Sidhe energies than it is to see the angels. At times, important land forms bear names of heroes or deities who embody sacred energies connected with the movements of various planets or stars, particularly at full moon or sunrise. In reality we know little about what really resides deep within the earth. Geoscience as an academic discipline is a relatively new science and naturally adopts a very linear way of perceiving the deep mysteries of the Earth. According to those who study the earth in a more mystical manner there is a wider paradigm in which everything on Earth is connected to the Greater Whole. The energies of the inner earth carry the imprint of distant planets and stars. When reading Maia Nartoomid's prolific works (2) for instance, we learnt that the essence of a far star can be stored deep within the earth, emerging when the time is right. As far as I understand it, the states of being she describes are seen with her soul and inner eye, and they equate to larger galactic events that scientists have not been able to fathom out yet. I gradually realised that her forays into the inner earth are as deeply significant as her forays into the far heavens, and that subtle, invisible parts of the Earth as a planet resonate with other stars out there. More to the point, the descriptions link us to a higher reality that we can access when we journey to the interior of our minds. Tales of fairy palaces deep within the earth are found in many ancient cultures. In many ways both the mythical subterranean cities and celestial palaces of which mystics and myths speak are describing states of mind. They represent higher mental frequencies met in states of deep meditation. The Immram in the cycles of Irish mythology are poems written down in the Middle Ages that speak of numerous paradises and cities and islands met on sea voyages made by roving monks. Irish medievalist Máirín Ní Dhonnchada convincingly hypothesized when presenting at a meeting of Galway Archaeology Society that these poems are written as teaching materials, or spiritual guidance, for the monks. I sense that the immrams are meditation aids in discerning the various levels of inner worlds or states of being. In modern day mysticism the jargon term "light codes" describes the frequencies associated with these states of mind or being. I am talking here about very deep states of meditation. They also occur when a person relaxes and allows one's consciousness to expand naturally into other realms. Nature can facilitate this.

There are places on Earth that carry rare vibrations that people can sense, and there is a simple method that can be used to access the essence of any such place more powerfully. It requires simply responding with sounds that are neither melodic, nor pretty, but which feel true in the moment. Such intuitive toning can be an expansive, enriching experience. By expressing the voice in a series of ad hoc tones, a deeper and more intimate connection is somehow made between the Earth and the person. It might explain why the Aborigines called the energy lines that cross the earth "song lines". I sense that sound opens avenues of communication, allowing energy to flow freely between the human and nature realms. Perhaps the Sidhe respond to the sound, and it is they who open the avenues of perception by temporarily altering the normally unheeded earth frequencies.

For me, toning causes a feeling to arise in me, akin to what I sense in the presence of nature beings, elementals or fairies. Animals and other creatures are closer to the elementals than humans, as a rule. I spontaneously started toning with a group of seals on the Scottish coast once. By doing so I sensed a deep communication and love from them.

Light/colour is created at an even higher frequency than sound. I think this explains why fairies are often seen as shifting shapes of colours and lights. In the Tama Do Institute created by the instigator of Vibrational Healing, Fabien Maman, training in Shamanics is based on the belief that trees and other natural objects all possess a core sound, and that when a human echoes or recreates that sound a deeper bond naturally occurs between the human and her natural surrounds. I have experienced this on my own path. This gentle process of merging with nature is similar to what occurs spontaneously when sighting fairies.

While the expression of the land is a vital ingredient in fairy lore, there is a sister ingredient that lies in the powerful role of myth. Myths contain hidden clues to the universe. For example in the last chapter we looked at how the everlasting milk of a magical cow belonging to Lon the Smith can be likened to the Milky Way galaxy of stars. By regarding fairy magic as encompassing life's deepest mysteries we can start to unravel myth in new ways.

In mythology, the upper realms of the stars are mirrored inside the earth. Looking at galactic events, since 1995 the mother galaxy from which Earth was created has been moving into a new era of which Coleston Brown wrote "the ancient mysteries of the Milky Way are revivified and brought into harmony with the Polar and Zodiacal streams of spiritual energies". (3)

What are the ancient mysteries of the Milky Way? According to the ancient mysteries of the Earth, the Milky Way represents the Under Realm, and the primordial mysteries of the Risen Sun or threefold light which occurs when the midwinter solstice sun aligns closest with the centre of the Milky Way. It is an archetypal rebirth that holds significance for a vast tract of time. The Earth was conceived and born in the Milky Way and will be reborn there on a subtle level according to the dictates of the skies. This rebirth will be seen in a new light- it will not necessarily be physical.

Coleston Brown mentions how the 2012 oft-quoted Grand Cross stellar alignment was but one of a series of events spanning 245 years in which the Zodiacal elliptical and the fixed polar stars coincide and align in closer harmony (4). The earth is said to be aligned right now with our "galactic equator" and it is believed that such a position heralds a new consciousness for all human beings. In the last chapter I shall talk more about this.

Returning to the legend of the Glas Cow on Slieve na Glasha in the Burren, you may recall that there were seven streams of water that marked the ceaseless flowing of milk. If you go to the townland of Teeskagh and stand above these waterfalls and listen to the pouring of the waters, you may be stirred to imagine the energies of the Seven Sisters of the Pleiades within the Milky Way, streaming into the earth below you here. The Glas with her overflowing milk is more than likely a metaphor for the Milky Way. There is indeed something primeval about this plateau on Slieve na Glasha that I cannot adequately put into words. There is an air of regeneration to it too. Remember, walking a landscape sensitively can awaken sensations in people seeking to understand the land at a deeper level. Consider then Lon the smith, living out of view of the rest of the world for an indeterminate length of time. Sensing the time was right for a new consciousness to take hold in Ireland, he presented himself to the world. He sacrificed his own people at the hands of the seven swords he himself had crafted. I have the notion that the striking of the swords mirrors the mystical power of the Pleiades being struck or even re-ignited. The Pleiades (together with Orion and Sirius) are a major co-creating influence in the new shift taking place today. The Milky Way is associated with the undying land and the isle of the blessed, and also the mysteries of the Underworld where deep celestial influences stir. Small wonder that Lon the keeper of the fairy De Danaan traditions lived on in a subterranean dwelling for hundreds of years, in the place where the seven streams/stars were born within the terrestrial Milky Way….he is the Keeper of Aeons.

Lon's occupation as a smith also bears significance. His female counterpart is Brigid, a saint derived from the earlier pagan goddess Bride or Brigid. Originally Brigid was an ancient triple goddess who embodied the qualities of poetry, healing and smithing. Her famous well dedication near Liscannor just south of the Burren is a pre-Christian site. St Brigid's feast day is the first day of the Celtic spring- Imbolc on Febuary 1st. Folk gather there then and also on the feast of Lughnasa, named after the god of smiths and artisans - known locally as Garland Sunday, which falls on the last Sunday in July each year. How interesting that the region's two main feast days are dedicated to the god and goddess of smithing! Smithing was held in high regard during the Celtic period.

Smiths were the sacred and secret keepers of tradition in many societies in ancient times. For instance, in Freemasonry the craft stems from ancient Egyptian times when the smith was the chief initiate, who held the key to knowledge which the civilization depended upon for its spiritual survival and wellbeing. The power of the celestial skies was transformed into practical affairs by understanding the alchemical mysteries. The shamanic medieval smith who experienced the mysteries on behalf of the tribe could change reality for all, like a talisman. Working with matter from deep within the earth, the smith in effect was transforming stellar matter (as represented by the precious metals).

What are the summary active ingredients in a fairy landscape such as Slieve na Glasha? In relation to the forces of the earth and skies, I see Lon as a kind of pole star round which the other stars revolve. He is at the centre of the Zodiac and its changing patterns. At the sunrise of our winter solstice there is a beautiful vesica pisces forming as the our pole star Lon and his beautiful cow Glasha, alias the Milky Way, intersect and interact. When the zodiacal stars draw near to their galactic centre in the Milky Way, as they do around now, the stellar forces contained in the earth form a new star. Simultaneously the dragon lines, that have been lying dormant for so long, now draw inwards to the centre of the earth, gathering in strength and intensity. The legend has echoes of the stellar orientations at the centre of our galaxy. Now is the time that the dragon returns centre stage! In its journey home we can expect chaos on the surface, as everything clumsily realigns to the new paradigm.

The higher Sidhe energies were used in traditional alchemy, an ancient healing art. This was referenced in the writings of those relatively modern mystics of the Celtic Revival in Ireland, who lived close to the Burren at the turn of the twentieth century. It is one thing to write about such things. It is quite another to experience the energies directly.

1. Eternal Elements 2010 Jackie Queally ISBN 978-0954143565 http://www.celtictrails.co.uk/books-for-sale-2/
2. www.spiritmythos.org
3 Secrets of a Fairy Landscape 2012 Coleston Brown Green Fire ISBN 978-0-9865912208 p59
4. Secrets of a Fairy Landscape 2012 Coleston Brown Green Fire ISBN 978-0-9865912208 P70

Element Four

SPIRIT OF EARTH

Concluding remarks: The element of Fire supports the Earth element, that is shared with the elementals, or nature spirits. There are various names, in various cultures, for the nature spirits who have many subdivisions. In Ireland, the generic name for these spirits is the Sidhe (pronounced "shee"), and often where Christians "colonised" an area place-names reflected the old pantheon of nature gods and spirits which were renamed after saint associations. In our modern era, the qualities of the fairies and other spirits are often overlooked. They hold the space for stellar and other cosmic energies to reside within the earth. The above chapter on the Spirit of Sidhe honours them and talks of specific areas and events in the Burren that reflect their magic. Now it is time to turn to the angelic realms, and to reflect upon the stars and cosmos more.

Element 5: Spirit of Metal/Ether

Juxtaposed
Pagan needle and Christian cross
Or would it be monk's folly and pagan cross?
United in witnessing
The passage of time.
Yet the endless energies
Pour through an invisible spout.
The tower receives as much
As the circle completes
An endless cycle.

Element Four

Chapter 6 Round Towers as Geomantic Boosters

The energies of the cosmos are twinned with the high sidhe energies of the Earth as a planet, which is placed within a wider galactic system. Round towers are manifold in Ireland and are connected to cosmic energies. They cannot be neglected in our study of the Burren and surrounding area. Ireland's tallest mainland round tower flanks the eastern fringes of the Burren, and serves to further boost the energies of a wide area. Work by Professor Callahan and other researchers into electro-magnetic fields will be profiled, as they "cracked the code" somewhat as to the subtle functions and effects of these enigmatic structures. This chapter is devoted to exploring the nature of round towers and introduces the element of metal/ether continued in the next chapter.

The patterning in the Burren earth grid displays close parallels with a very rare form of sacred geometry known as the Reshel. Its chief proponent William Buehler, an esteemed mystic and retired Naval commander, taught me how to interpret grids that hold specific functions in the etheric (non-visible layer of energy). Remember that grids are in effect complex thought forms, or states of being, represented in three dimensional forms. In terms of the Burren, this vast complex earth grid works on various levels with the divine energies present. Unsurprisingly perhaps, the pentagram is a key feature in the Burren grid. The grid seems to represent a state of being that is intermediate between a very divine state (as represented by Reshel grids) and our more limited state of being, where life is viewed from a three dimensional perspective here on Earth. There are intervening states of being between the two extremes and the grid resonates in that arena. Most significantly the grid indicates that the Burren is imbued with heavenly energies. That is why people find it such a spiritually nourishing place to be. The element of metal is represented by the earth grids and the round towers. In the physical realm metal slowly dissolves and releases its minerals into the water. When mineral-rich waters emerge in a pure spring, the water is often perceived as a holy well. Similarly on a more metaphysical level, our thoughts are stored in and carried by water. This brings us round the start of our cycle again.

In an early chapter we looked at how the element of wood can be likened to the new pioneering energies and thinking of the early monks. By comparison there is another quality of thinking which is fed by the Sidhe and the Earth element we just looked at. This thinking bears the qualities of metal. Subtle and mercurial, it can be expressed in geometrical patterns. As mentioned in the Spirit of Water, the patterns can be traced over the land, when they are known as earth grids. The grids reflect the cosmic force in the land. They are not physical patterns but etheric patterns, or grids, of underlying energies that influence human beings on subtle levels.

As a planet, the Earth pulsates with powerful rhythms of electrical and magnetic force in much the same way we do. We are affected by the Earth's pulse especially when we require inspiration – it is one of the reasons people travel to sacred sites, and also the reason that people relocate. Human beings require focus and willpower to sustain their endeavours and projects at times. Different locations vary in their subtle underlying qualities, and so one location will suit one individual more than another to dwell in. The land can subtly draw them to relocate. Then mundane events will transpire that cause a certain individual to move, although in the beginning it might have been triggered by their soul's need to evolve into a different vibration, which prompted them to seek out a new vibrational environment that suits them better.

Similarly the quality of an earth grid will often affect our human actions, without us realizing that location-specific events are often following pre-ordained patterns in the land. For instance, I knew a woman who unknowingly moved from one arm of a pentagram grid over Edinburgh to the next arm, in both instances living equidistant from the centre of the pentagram. Later she became aware of the overlaying grid and was quite surprised. It seemed to confirm how we often make a physical move in life and nothing inwardly changes. Since our inward states draw us to outer events that mirror our state of being, she moved within the same pattern in this instance. We carry our patterns inside us and move according the dictates of those patterns. In this instance she found the equivalent position in the same grid! Even broader historical events can follow grid patterns, or at least be influenced by the pattern.

A simple earth grid is a network of lines. It is not very clear what is being created as there may be no dynamic geometry involved. It is an earth grid nevertheless and has some limited potential. A grid has to be worked with at a conscious level in order to achieve anything in the 3D world. It is the the human imagination that unlocks the key to creating a powerful earth grid. Understandably such work lay until recently in the hands of holy people who were entrusted to act wisely. Nowadays the work can be done with altruistic love that will resonate with divine principles and bring harmony and healing to wherever it is needed, often a long distance off from the source. Earth grids need anchoring at specific points, or they merely float in the air and do not interact with the sentience of the Earth in order to assist its transformation. Once anchored the earth grid starts to gather momentum. Natural power points in the landscape can boost their efficacy. In this chapter, I introduce ancient monuments that act like acupuncture points within the meridians or leys of the land. Sometimes these leys are part of wider grids and other times they stand alone. When the acupuncture points are active the whole ley line, or ley system, becomes active and so many places are affected through association.

Speaking more specifically now, I sense that the round towers in Ireland perform like acupuncture command points. Since many of them lie in ruins, we may well ask whether their role is to some extent defunct due to a change in earth energies. Also it is important to note that the towers do not necessarily anchor an earth grid. They do ensure that the earth energies flow over a wide hinterland.

I have often noticed that when a grid is "active" and alive the towns or monuments on the grid thrive. (For a grid to be activated it merely requires someone to discover it, since they draw on information from the ether in order to create a grid. Conversely, without human recognition the grids lie dormant, or at least not so active).

In the vicinity of the Burren there is at least one round tower is intact, having been restored in the late nineteenth century to its full height of over 111 feet, complete with conical roof! The tower is at Kilmacduagh, which was founded by the local saint, Colman (mentioned in Chapter 3). It is the tallest mainland tower in Ireland and its location within the landscape is interesting to explore. The Burren is not just the visible mountain range to the west but also, as mentioned in Chapter 2 , the low lying land to the north east, known as the Gort Lowlands. It seems somehow fitting that the tower at Kilmacduagh is placed between two geologically distinct areas. To the west lies the Burren hills while to the east lies the rounded older Slieve Aughty Mountains past the market town of Gort. Thus the command point of Kilmacduagh straddles the female and male landscape energies. I believe that the round tower at Kilmacduagh plays an important role in spinning a high level etheric grid over this wider hinterland.

I was fortunate in my quest to understand the deeper raison d'être for building the tall monuments. I discovered the work of Professor Philip S. Callahan, a lateral-thinking academic whose mind is very probing. As an entomologist and natural philosopher he has recorded a spiralling of magnetic energies from Round Towers.

He published a definitive study of the magnetic life of agriculture in 1984. In addition in his book "Ancient Mysteries Modern Visions The Magnetic Life of Agriculture" he includes a most interesting map study (1) of the round towers in Ireland and their distribution. He correlated the star map of the northern skies over Ireland with the distribution of round towers to prove that they approximately reproduced the patterns of constellations in the night skies! Callahan uses some poetic licence to match with the local pattern of round towers (including Scattery Island). Draco is the most accurately represented by the distribution of round towers. To the immediate south below the dragon's tail lies the Burren. (The Big Dipper is slightly misplaced to the east of its stellar position.)

Somehow, when studying the Big Dipper formation on his map, I associate it with the mysterious crop formation phenomena occurring worldwide now. I am reminded of a crop circle formation that appeared in 2008 in England. The pattern started with a large insect head, to which a body was added the following night. Then on the subsequent night, long mysterious lettering appeared, dangling from the tail of its body! In a similar vein, due to the more easterly positioning of the Big Dipper it appears as though the round towers at Kilnaboy and Dysart O'Dea are extensions of the long tail of the dragon Draco. They would lie in the path of such coding were the dragon a crop circle!

Kilmacduagh is significantly positioned, where the handle of the Big Dipper meets the cup, and on further examining the star map, I

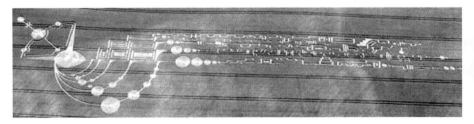

found interesting connections with other round towers. For instance, Clonmacnoise is said to be Polaris the Pole Star by which we determine our north. Clonmacnoise was a major Christian centre in Ireland during the Golden Age of Celtic Christianity. Sailing up the Shannon one year, the first sighting of Clonmacnoise took my breath away. Majestically poised on the river bank, it looks as though it is rooted there from time immemorial. I had arrived at the North Star, rather than the North pole, so to speak! By drawing a line from there to the Big Dipper and extending it on Callahan's map one reaches Denebelo in Leo, a very important star for incoming cosmo-spiritual energies. Mystics say it is where the New Earth Star will emerge – it seats the consciousness of a new future version of our own planet.

Whilst Callahan might have used some imagination in sketching his star map to correlate with the distribution of round towers, his research into the rare subject of "paramagnetism" in relation to these monuments is both unique and very accurate. He noted that the round towers were a common part of monastic complexes built mainly in the sixth century. He likens the man-made towers to the way that antennae perform in insect behaviour. Both the towers and insect antennae are able to resonate with and amplify extremely low frequency (ELF) electro-magnetic waves.

Electrical engineer Kieran Comerford (2) interestingly points out that these ELF waves are produced in the earth's atmosphere by a resonance phenomenon. There is a cavity between the earth's surface and the ionosphere that acts as a resonator to ELF waves of 7.83 Hz with additional harmonics at 14, 20, 26 and 33 Hz. These frequencies exactly match our EEG brain frequencies, with the alpha waves commonly produced in meditation states being set to the 7.83 Hz, also known as the Schumann resonance. Referring to Callahan's research, Comerford postulates that any magnetic energy flowing down a round tower produces a "magnetic vector potential" that concentrates healing energy on the spot.

Callahan maintains these towers were built to accumulate and disperse these positive energies at extremely low frequencies that he calls "paramagnetic" forces. As a seasoned researcher Comerford agrees that the so-called paramagnetic qualities of the stone tower itself may help to tune the incoming energy to resonate with the Schumann Resonance. In his fascinating and unique book "Ancient Mysteries Modern Visions", Callahan outlines a process in magneto-electricity whereby the towers act like giant antennae for magnetic particles of subtle energy released from solar flare activity and the atmosphere. All particles that are weakly repellent to magnetism are "diamagnetic" and absorbed by plants and trees, whereas the paramagnetic particles are held in the soil and contribute to healthy crop growth. It is one of the reasons why monasteries built the towers, so as to ensure healthy food production levels! Accordingly stone mountains such as exist in the Burren would act in a similar manner. Certainly the soil pockets are rich in the Burren, but not on the scale that modern farming favours!

The towers often have rubble infill to varying degrees inside them and Callahan maintains this serves to fine-tune the tower, so it can receive the exact level of cosmic rays it needs(3). The towers were tuned to low level microwave radiation present in the night sky. In the day time they emit the beneficial cosmic rays to the environment around. In short, the surrounding trees (of which there were many at the time it was built) attract diamagnetic energies while the tower both stores and emits paramagnetic (mildly magnetic) energies into the wider environment. (Incidentally Callahan believes that natural healers have more paramagnetic energy than other people. It is this energy they use to heal with.)y

The powers accumulate around the doors. It is interesting to note that the one at Kilmacduagh is set at over 26 feet above ground, making it the highest of all Irish round towers. Presumably the magneto-electrical energies are more prolific at a greater height there, and the tower is geared to collecting these energies at quite a distance above the ground. With such a tall doorway and overall height of tower I would imagine that the subtle energies are distributed over a far greater hinterland than normally occurs with round towers. It would also make it harder to feel the energies at ground level. When I started out dowsing with pendulums and rods I realised that I must have been dowsing the land with my whole body all my life, for I sensed vibrations attracting and affecting people on the land. When I learnt how to dowse I realised that this art brought my intuitive faculties into sharper focus. I can dowse the door and window openings when walking round, when I set the intent to do so. The instant buzz that I can get when passing towers is more evasive at Kilmacduagh though, and I find it really more tangible when the sun breaks through on a rare hot day! Burke and Halberg (4) claim that the higher the stone above ground, the more ions it interacts with. Tall stones are able to conduct airborne ions on any pathway.

What must not be overlooked here is the fact that such energies spiral out from the tower and are not fixed to one direction when emitted. I respect and believe Callahan's theories, especially since he has conducted experiments with plants to prove the effects of planting near round towers with conical roofs intact. One evening, with five quizzical onlookers present, I conducted an experiment he recommended, using a model of the round tower and a powerful magnet. Eventually having stripped out all possible variables on our results, we were able to generate a repellent magnetic field that caused the tower to spin on it axis by placing the magnet at a short distance away from the model! This to me proves that the energies can spin out from the tower since the tower itself cannot spin in its 3D situation!

I also ponder on the position of Kilmacduagh at the north east edge of the Burren, because when buildings were used by spiritual adepts, they regarded the north east as the main pole for downloading spiritual energies within the eight cardinal directions. That is the reason why Stonehenge and Chartres Cathedral are oriented north east. It is perhaps fitting that Ireland's tallest tower is positioned in the northeast corner of Ireland's most magnetically potent area. Furthermore I see its position as pivotal to the area, since it lies between what I call the Backbone of the Burren (with its landmark topography) and the lower lying older Gort Lowlands that I call the Underbelly. It is this region that digests the energies and recycles the memory of the lands through its rivers, weaving under and above the worn surface of the land. A sparrow's hop further northeast lies Coole Park, former home to Lady Gregory who co-founded the Abbey Theatre in Dublin, early last century. She was a great supporter of the Irish arts, in particular literature. She collected much folklore, an interest keenly felt by her protégé WB Yeats, who bought another tower nearby known as Thor Ballylee. The sponsoring of a healthy revival in Ireland's indigenous culture was spawned in the Gort Lowlands, an area of fast flowing underground rivers and disappearing lakes or turloughs as they are called. The area was very rich in folklore once, and in many ways the true Celtic spirit thrived in these lands, aided by philanthropic local landlords who bucked the trend of English cruelty, way ahead of their times. The whole area is enchanting and beguiling in her femininity and fertility, whereas the broody male Slieve Aughtys, with their denser more acid soils, observe her dance from a short distance.

Whilst Kilmacduagh's round tower is perched on the north eastern flanks of the Burren, by contrast Scattery Island's round tower lies to the southwest of the Burren, serving the less ostentatious shales of West Clare: close cousins of the Burren, since the limestone present in the Burren lies below these more recent shale deposits. I include Scattery in this book on the Burren since I feel it is rather neglected and has a right to be honoured.

On the tower at Kilmacduagh there are six windows at regular intervals, level with the eaves - this according to meta scientist William Buehler would energetically make a strong connection to the divine heart energies in the cosmos. In Hebrew gematria the number 6 acts as the main connective between realms. It also is the best number for making connections with all systems of energies. So it is a perfect number of window openings to facilitate energetic connections with other places. Since Callahan's scientific model suggested that rare solar particles are collected by the tower, then there is a subtle reference to Christ here, who many see as the Sun or chief life force, as well as the divine heart.

The lower windows are placed at erratic intervals around the tower, as if to align with aerial ley lines of varying frequencies that would emit the electro-magnetic wavelengths quite a distance. Due to the tower being filled with rubble inside to several feet, I believe it is harder to pick up these leys compared to other structures that emit their rays at ground level. The infilling is crucial though for fine-tuning the energies so that the tower can best process the subtle cosmic energies. The five degree leaning aspect of the tower might have been deliberate too. There is much we do not know about para-magnetic energies!

The elegant and almost haunting round tower of Kilmacduagh is said to have been built in the tenth century, but some local farmers believe it was built far earlier. For instance, St Colman the founder of Kilmacduagh had a brother St Caimin, who lived on Holy Island in Lough Derg in east Clare. He is said to have built the round tower there. It remains a shadow of what it was and yet is very powerful to dowse, partly as its door is not set high like at Kilmacduagh. St Colman is said to have died in 630 and St Caimin in 653. If it is true then this adds weight to the round tower at Kilmacduagh having been built far earlier.

The round tower on Scattery Island was built first by St Senan (488-560) and was unfinished according to local lore. (Again it suggests that the round towers were built far earlier than the ninth or tenth century.) In later times the Scattery tower was completed and it is said to have reached 120 feet, making it higher than Kilmacduagh and the tallest of all Irish towers. Its door lies near sea level, which means that there was no need to bank up to the doorway with infill - the ground height works perfectly for any leys that operate here, and would be easily detected when dowsing. According to Callahan there was a 2-4 times increase in electromagnetic low frequency (ELF) waves i.e. 8-2 HZ that were strongest at dawn and dusk within the tower when he measured it. Considering that the tower is positioned with no infill and the door is at ground level it suggests the height of the island was perfect for the function of the tower, which did not need adjusting in order to gather powerful cosmic rays and disperse any leys. This might account for the mythical tunnel going from Holy Island to Scattery Island, and the serpent energy is said to flow up the Shannon to Scattery; the island was perfectly placed.

Some say that these round towers were really built as a local effort to stave off Viking invasion? Anyone could easily torch a tower, seal the only doorway and trap all the inhabitants on the wooden floors within. Long before I read Professor Callahan's book, I had an intuitive understanding of how these towers work. I believed, from studying and experiencing the energies of Abernethy Round Tower in Scotland, that there was a practical yet spiritual reason that humans built these towers as follows: Abernethy in Fife had been a Culdee stronghold and was the centre of faith for the southern Picts in early times. Luckily the tower has a spiral staircase in it so I was able to climb inside and from the positioning of corbel stones note the points at where floors once had lain. When I vertically dowsed it, as I climbed the pendulum would move in response to each floor level. (Such corbels were detected at Scattery Island too in the eighteenth century (5).

My dowsing confirmed that the floors correlated with a series of energy points or chakras we have in our own body. In fact the towers were built as meditation aids, so that the monks could tune into each chakra level as they sat on different floor levels of the tower. In geomancy, people often overlook the fact that energies are anchored vertically as well as horizontally. When Rosslyn Chapel had an external gantry visitors could climb, they had access to these vertical energies. Often sensitive visitors experienced and acknowledged higher energies that they were not exposed to when entering the chapel at ground level. This would explain why there were so few windows in round towers since views were not paramount for meditation. The floors within the round towers worked together to provide veritable meditation vessels where the monks could do internal work, working with their different chakras. As they sat meditating their energy or light bodies would expand, much in the same way that the Earth as a sentient being is in an expanded mode at a sacred site. The monks could well have been tuning into the site in order to experience the increased energy field there- the chakra system is linked to the energy field. A human being downloads information through the crown chakra yet does not tune into this energy all the time since this would give rise to imbalance. Even writing a book like this which focuses on non-physical phenomena requires me to stay grounded. I have always found I could focus on the higher frequencies of the spiritual worlds if I balanced that activity with something that is either of the Earth or in my body, such as giving a massage, singing, gardening or collecting herbs in the wild. By working both ends of the chakra spectrum I can keep the flow going best. In the same way it is impractical to perceive the whole of the earth vibrating at this high level constantly as it would be too much for our current senses to cope with. Some souls are drawn to clearing the Earth of lower levels of perceived sufferings endured at the hands of humans often. According to mystics I trust this is more for their own healing and development, since the Earth has a great capacity to heal itself and will survive beyond our own survival!

Burke and Halberg have investigated fluctuations in electro-magnetism produced especially along areas of "conductivity discontinuity" that can have dramatic effects on the human brain. They identified electrically active spots where drier or less metallic rocks meet limestone areas. (This activity can also occur within fluctuating types of limestone within an essentially limestone area). I am stating this here as a possibility that I cannot prove as I have no scientific measuring instruments to apply to the local landscape. Were it the case it would certainly enhance the tower's properties for use as a serial meditation chamber. Nearby in various directions the land does change dramatically back to surface limestone.

Perhaps the pile of infill helped to avoid a likely lightning strike on their structures. Burke and Halberg explain that tall stone structures tend to interact with more positive ions in the air and even conduct them along selected pathways in the air. (6) How does it work? The negative ions held in the ground at Kilmacduagh would travel up the limestone tower, particularly if there are trace elements of metals such as iron in the stone. Electrons will escape in an electron shower from its pointed conical roof and cause ionization in the air. When the positive ions in the air meet the electrons they are neutralized, and elements such as nitrogen in the air will turn into nitrates; a form of nitrogen readily usable by cereal plants. If this natural airborne fertilizer is carried downwind to the area which the plants are growing then there is marked beneficial effect on their growth and yield (7). Their conclusions seem to echo what occurred in Callahan's experiments. They write of "electron showers" that are good for seed growth and fertility of soil. Their research discovered that planting seeds inside ancient mounds increased plant vitality and improved the plants' ability to cope with stress. It begs the question whether the Irish round towers were used for this purpose! Certainly the monasteries became significant centres of local food production.

On a contrary note, in areas where round towers exist the folk belief has been prevalent that one was safe from a lightning strike in the vicinity of the tower. It begs the question as to whether folk believed the tower would attract the strike or whether the whole area, including the tower itself, was immune from a strike. The latter would augment the above theory since normally lightning occurs when negatively charged particles sweep down to earth to meet positively charged particles rising from ground level along upright objects. Unlike trees that emit positive charges, the tower is acting otherwise. If the tower is emitting negatively charged particles this negates the normal lightning process. This whole area is inconclusive and open to debate: here I have simply tried to describe what research has to say about the matter of round towers.

I have always been attracted to the islands that host round towers. What exactly is the nature of islands like Scattery Island and Holy Island? There seems to be a deep spiritual function at play I shall attempt to explain. Again, acknowledgement is due to William Buehler for the explanation of the dynamics, only part of which I was able to discern before consulting this living oracle!

When we get outside of a temporal state, to which time belongs, we enter a causal state of being in which there are no polarities. The sea is a mass of water carrying non-polarized codes in energetic terms. Water has the capacity to hold memory and so although the state of being of water is said to be non-polarized it provides the basis for thoughts and later actions, since form follows thought. The actions primarily take place on the land, and are seen as a female in function, as the female gestates form. She responds to the male thought forms which are inseminating the constantly changing flow of energy, conditioning and organising it too. In a simple way, the sea contains within it a male function of "no form" or "being formless" that is translated into "form" by the female presence the Earth. The sea requires control centres to accept the non-polarized charge of the water and translate it into something in the temporal i.e. tangible realm. Islands with towers carry special functions in that they act as transmitters of the sea codes, or thought forms, passing them onto the land where they are translated into appropriate action, associated with the divine creative codes or energies held within the mass of water.

Since much of Ireland is boggy and wet, the inland towers are always close to non-polarized bodies of water that perform similarly to the sea. When we look at the function of these inland towers I believe that something similar is occurring as at sea: when non polarized solar particles are emitted from round towers the atmosphere becomes a non-polarized state in which the round towers act like antennae serving to anchor the solar energies on the land. I view all round towers as demarcating acupuncture points on meridians (leys) of the land. The solar energies are then carried along leys to other places, rather like the dragon lines carry information over vast distances.

Finally, perhaps you now can see why temples of many religions always have water features within their design, or are placed near either the sea or a lake, as then the energies are balanced and can continually upgrade on a spiritual level.

1. Ancient Mysteries Modern Visions The Magnetic Life of Agriculture Philip Callahan PhD 2001 Acres USA ISBN 0-911311 diagram and explanation p108
2. Newgrange and the New Science 2011 CTM Books www.kcomerford.com p 143
3. Ancient Mysteries Modern Visions The Magnetic Life of Agriculture Philip Callahan PhD 2001 Acres USA ISBN 0-911311 diagram and explanation p25
4. Seeds of Knowledge Stone of Plenty 2005 John Burke and Kaj Halberg Council Oak Books ISBN 1-57178-184-6 p?
5. The Stranger's gaze Travels in County Clare 1534-1950 1198 Clasp Press ed Brian O'Dalaigh ISBN 1 900545 08x p 142
6. Seeds of Knowledge Stone of Plenty 2005 John Burke and Kaj Halberg Council Oak Books ISBN 1-57178-184-6 p138
7 ibid p138

Metal/Ether

SPIRIT OF METAL/ETHER (in relation to round towers)

Concluding remarks: Round towers are connected to cosmic energies that cannot be neglected in our study. The energies of the cosmos are twinned with the high Sidhe energies of the Earth as a planet within a wider galactic system. Ireland's tallest mainland round tower flanks the eastern fringes of the Burren, and serves to further boost the energies of a wide area. Work by Professor Callahan (4) and other researchers into electro-magnetic fields were profiled as they "cracked the code" somewhat as to the subtle functions and effects of these enigmatic structures. This chapter has been devoted to exploring the nature of round towers and supplements the element of metal/ether described in the next chapter.

Element 5: Element of Metal (Ether)

DOONAGORE
Invisible pointer
To a world beyond
Mirrored in your fairy tale
Miraculously splashed on an Atlantic palette
Of blues and greys and greens.

Element Four

Chapter 7 Leys and Earth Grids

The Earth yields minerals to the rocks which form various metals in its seams. The gnomic Sidhe assist the long processes that metals undergo in their formation.

On a non-physical level, the metal element is expressed in the ether and in man's intellectual processes, when he uses mind in a dense and focussed manner, as opposed to the watery processes of dreaming and imagining that precede concrete thought. Imagine that intellectual processes can be expressed in terms of sacred geometry, not just in two dimensional forms but also in three, even four dimensional forms and beyond! Sacred geometry has the capability to serve as coding for complex thought patterns. (Often when I write I doodle patterns. They probably are reflecting my current state of mind, before I hopefully shift to a concrete final thought I can communicate! Thoughts can be represented by two dimensional patterns on paper, but in a higher reality they occupy space and therefore are at least three dimensional.)

When thought patterns emanate from a pure or divine source they too can express themselves in sacred geometry. Then the thought form becomes more akin to a state of being. These patterns involving sacred geometry can be traced in churches and other sacred structures. When creating any sacred space such as a church, sacred geometry and skills in geomancy overlapped within building design and layout. For instance, there were geomancers in the Middle Ages who sited buildings according to natural laws that would encourage good fortune. Then one site often was connected to another sacred site by either following current existing leys or even creating new leys by thought intent under divine guidance. In other words, leys are a product of mental projection aligned with divine energies. They can even be installed by mere mental recognition if one is in a meditative state of being. The early saints would have walked these leys from one cell to another, constructing small "churches" to pray in close to the holy wells. In yet earlier times forts, cairns and graves of various kinds were placed on the leys, upon which early rituals may have taken place. When the leys combine to form discernible patterns overlaying the land,

modern day geometers can detect these "earth grids".
The web of leys cast over the land may be rooted within the earth or
be more aligned with cosmic forces above the earth's surface. Grids vary
enormously in how they are formed.

Since abstract geometric patterns essentially represent thought forms, the
patterns can underpin many phenomena – and these thought forms present
themselves as "earth grids" in the landscape. These grids consist of leys of
varying mental qualities. This is because leys perform a variety of functions
that are both man-made and natural, of which the former are infused to
greater or lesser extent with divine energies. Natural leys more consistently
carry a deep resonance with the divine creator whilst man-made ones will
inevitably vary in energetic frequency. There is more than one layer of
ley line patterns in the Burren. The patterns created by ley lines are to be
differentiated from the natural dragon leys mentioned in Chapter 2. Leys
can be detected as alignments between monuments and other landmarks,
or they can even be lines that connect natural features such as hilltops.
When the leys connect to one another and display beautiful patterns of
sacred geometry that impact on one another like cogs in a wheel, one gets a
sense that the energy is active in the land. The patterns are generally known
as earth grids by geometers and geomancers who were skilled in their
understanding of earth energies rather in the manner that experts in Feng
Shui operate today.

As stated earlier, the act of human recognition of a grid is enough to "install
it" or bring it into being! This is because in the etheric world everything
is created by thought. Anything that comes into being our consciousness
spontaneously comes into etheric existence. I used to wonder if the grids
we discern nowadays exist haphazardly or if earlier geomancers had already
accurately surveyed the land and projected these grids to build sites on.
Alternatively, perhaps the settlers had exercised their extra-sensory faculties
when they discovered the patterns? After several years observing others
discover earth grids I believe now that these grids can already exist with no
prior human intervention, but equally the grids can be created by mental
projection. It is quite astounding that Earth and human consciousness
interact on the non-physical level in a two way process. Sometimes I have
sensed a ley come into being as I dowse, and it has been quite disorientating
as I wondered if the ley was coming into my consciousness as I dowsed,

or whether I was creating it by the very act of walking sensitively with a dowsing pendulum! The two way connection we have with our planet is largely overlooked in everyday society because it requires practice and patience to understand how it works.

I first discovered that ley lines in the land can create patterns of sacred geometry when I was devising tours in Scotland. I was selecting specific sites for their historical relationship with one another, while unbeknown to me there was an undercurrent of invisible patterns in the landscape that the sites adhered to. I realized that certain groups, such as the Knights Templar and the Cistercians, would build their burial sites or their monasteries on the nodes of sacred geometry within these patterns. The geomantic art of detecting leys and determining sites for ceremonies is a rather neglected skill.

I have acquired extensive experience "working" with ley lines and earth grids, and am fairly familiar with the way they work. The earth grids consist of a patterning of straight leys that the earth's wavy (dragon) leys will inevitably boost when the two respective paths cross. The Australian Aborigines still walk their leys, and name them song lines because they can sense the vibrations that ley lines emit. Sensitive people the world over can perceive these lines in various ways. Dowsing/divining with rods or a pendulum is one method of tuning into them. Geomantic knowledge is an essential ingredient in the spiritual interpretation of landscapes, and the Burren has a fascinating earth grid and an implied role to play that I will describe in the final chapter.

Before focussing on local ley lines, it might be helpful to try and trace the energetic link between earth energies and human consciousness, starting from a more physical viewpoint. Physics is not an easy subject for me to write about, but I will begin with a tentative exploration of what might be influencing what is generally known as earth energies. I will then go on to discuss more metaphysical aspects of earth energies, for those readers who are more interested in the spiritual aspects.

As far as I understand there is a geomagnetic field around the Earth which protects life on Earth from ultra-violet rays, deflecting solar winds and other particles of high electrical energy from the sun. Meanwhile, within the earth there is a subtle intertwining of electricity and magnetism which creates geomagnetic forces. These forces are known as telluric currents, which form ley lines when channelled into straight, or wavy, lines that dowsers and geomancers detect, using their rods or pendulums. The ley lines often join nodes on the earth's surface where underground forces reach the surface.

Incidentally there is iron at the molten core of the earth that influences these leys. Iron affects the Earth's magnetic field. Iron is also a crucial component for both our blood and our brains. Within the sinuses of the ethmoid bone at the base of our skulls (above the nose in a cavity between the two orbits or eye sockets) we actually possess pyramid-shaped miniscule crystals of magnetite that can detect the Earth's magnetic field. (1) Since bones carry an electrical charge in their crystalline structure, electro magnetism affects human bodies. Anne Silk (2) remarked that humankind has two additional senses for survival in modern times: electricity and magnetism. In addition to being present within the ethmoid sinus, she adds that "magnetosomes" exist in the brain, thymus, lungs, spleen, liver and blood haem. The most magneto-sensitive parts of the body are the pineal, hypothalamus, Ammon's Horn in the hippocampus and the aforementioned ethmoid sinus. Their sensitivity impacts on our ability to dowse ley lines and sense direction.

Electricity and magnetism are interlinked. Moving electric currents generate magnetic fields, and whenever a magnetic field changes, more electrical currents are produced in anything that will conduct that current.

In the Burren, we have a vast area of limestone that is quite impervious to water but which abundant rainwater has dissolved over time. The water works its way through the many natural fissures in the rock and so does not remain on the surface. Underneath the water behaves erratically, for instance becoming a fast flowing waterfall one minute and then broadening out into a wide slow-flowing stream for a while. Water is positively charged. The limestone surface is negatively charged. As water moves through the rock, the surface is charged with energy due to the interaction of positive and negative molecules occurring. In addition water serves to generate a magnetic field (3). Since the water changes its volume according to the rainfall, daily fluctuations in magnetism will occur. According to Burke and Halberg (4) further electrical currents are generated by these magnetic changes.

Meanwhile on the surface we have to consider the type of limestone that exists here. It is an oolitic limestone, meaning it consists of small egg-shaped particles of calcite wrapped around organic oceanic matter and sand (quartz). Early cultures regarded such limestone as sacred due to it holding millions of years of earthly life forms within its structure (5). Researcher Paul

Devereux found that the earth temples in Avebury used oolitic limestone in their Neolithic barrows (6).As already mentioned in the previous chapter, Professor Callahan discovered that the oolitic limestone variety is highly paramagnetic and so is attracted to a magnetic field. This means that the oolitic limestone will combine well with the water and create a charged landscape. It is also the reason the round towers are specifically built of this type of limestone, since they will act like a magnet to attract cosmic energies. Interestingly Irish dwellings are usually made of diamagnetic (mildly repelled by a magnetic field) insulating material from the limestone found in great central plain of Ireland (7). It is worth considering the structures of the Great Pyramid, which is constructed with limestone layers. A layer of paramagnetic limestone is encased within the more common and less pure diamagnetic limestone, which serves to insulate a structure so as to accumulate cosmic energy drawn in through the capstone whose stone would be high in magnetic content. Iron and other trace elements are found in the local limestone of the Burren. It appears that the Round Towers are constructed in reverse, with the magnetic stones on the exterior and the diamagnetic material on the interior at base level. This would indicate the energies are dispersed rather than contained. It would be well worth analysing the stone qualities of the Round Towers for their properties to see if they adhere to any patterns. Certainly these enigmatic structures deserve more serious attention, as it is hard to believe that, built as they were within monastic settings of great learning, the magnetic properties of their mode of construction was simply accidental.

In summary, we can expect frequent energy boosts (electrical charges) in the Burren, with its ubiquitous underground waters. We can also expect an amplified magnetic field, which in turn attracts rare cosmic energies because oolitic limestone will, under certain conditions, amplify cosmic paramagnetic energies.

In the Burren, the natural limestone escarpments are one of the most potent features of its landscape. In the Slieve na Glasha legend, the cow slept close to the edge of such an escarpment. Heavier positive ions are produced along escarpments in the rock, according to Burke and Halberg. There is an actual fault line lying close to the edge of the cliff. Again according to Burke and Halberg, magnetic anomalies can be expected along the edge of fault lines in much in the same way as their "conductivity discontinuities" occur (8). It creates a powerful place to sit and soak in the positive ions - this might well be the reason the Cow at Slieve na Glasha did not move off each day from the spot close to the cliffs, since the increase in energy may well have affected her milk yield! There is no smoke without fire to these ancient legends...the seven streams tumble down over the fault line too!

In the hermitage that St Colman lived in below Eagle's Rock there is a definite northeast orientated fault line running parallel to the cliff escarpment. Again it is interesting to note the orientation as this occurs on a larger scale in Scotland with the long fault line running through Loch Ness where the large elemental form of Nessie has been oft times spotted!

In the hidden cave of Glencurran, a little to the east of Slieve na Glasha, archaeologist Marion Dowd discovered a Bronze Age cairn structure with ritual objects such as perforated cowrie shells, unburnt remains of a child including its skull and neonatal bone deposit. Some of the finds are symbols of regeneration and rebirth that were often placed at burial sites. Bones have been found under the dolmens (giant table-shaped tombs) of the Burren and elsewhere in Ireland but the presence of a cairn within a cave is very rare. Glencurran lies at the junction of the limestone rocks and the less porous shale. There is a local fault line here that the cave entrance lies on. This together with calcite present will create a higher electrical charge in the air adjacent to it. Another factor to consider is that ground currents of electrical charges have been tested, and proved to be stronger inside chambers. All this might explain why when exiting the cave someone took a photograph of me and there was a massive pink ball of light hovering beside me. Electro-magnetic charges can appear as balls of light, or orbs, on digital photos.

I have never been able to photograph or witness orbs at Kilmacduagh. In a bid to discover more about its position outside of Gort, I took a GPS reading for the tower and measured the orientation of the door. I discovered that it led to Lindisfarne, a holy island off the north east coast of England, close to the Scottish border. The connection with Lindisfarne is fascinating and leads us into the more metaphysical realms, and leads us back to the Reshel ley system I am familiar with.

Lindisfarne is alternatively called Holy Island. A tidal island once belonging to Northumbria, it was closely linked to the abbey on Iona. In around the seventh century CE the Celtic monks from Lindisfarne Abbey, together with the local princes' sons, received their education there. It appears from mystic William Buehler's research that these early monks

Millenium statue in Lindisfarne Abbey

tapped into, on some level, the "Reshel" earth grids that exist. These earth grids are connecting to a range of energetic frequencies that lie far beyond what scientific instruments can measure-they lay beyond the known electro-magnetic field that even embrace the torshin fields that science is discovering. Buehler imagines the earth encased in an "Oritronic realm" beyond which lies the "Metatronic realm" of higher consciousness. His leys and earth grids relate to this higher frequency field. Their spiritual function is to assist, support and even create a new state of being overseen by archangel Metatron on a wider universe scale. A sheath surrounds the earth that shields humanity and all sentient life from direct exposure to the core vibrations of the Metatronic realm, since its frequencies are too high for us to cope with in our present state of being. At times this vibrant, Metatronic state reveals itself to humans, perhaps as part of a Shamanic retreat or journey or even when taking a casual walk in nature.

The isle of Iona in the Inner Hebrides in Scotland is a place where visitors feel their souls are deeply touched, as the veil is thin between realms there. I personally have found it to be so. Years ago Buehler explained that there was an extremely high frequency ley system going from Iona to Lindisfarne. He reckons that its purpose has evolved from when he first noticed it. Once it used to bring spiritual energies that he calls "light codes" into Matter, and then upload the transformed matter back to Spirit in a two-way flow. This affected human consciousness and the action as related to the constant recycling of human karmic action. The ley has now evolved into creating new blood and shedding forever the old outworn blood... in other words it is continually adjusting the DNA of new human race consciousness and is no longer concerned with karma. Changes are taking place on a spiritual level that does not allow time to wait for karma to play out. Now is the time for people to receive infusions of Christic energies. If one believes that, then it would mean that any other grid that connects with Lindisfarne will, at some level, be connected with new light codes.

The Reshel earth grids are to support the evolution of sentient beings. It was a privilege for me to intensely share Buehler's research for many years, as his work is borne by deep inner experiences generated in his "synergy light work" group. He has built up a composite picture of the inner realms concerned with creation. He consistently added to his research as systems upgrade. The work is very intense, and always starts with the still point, or Selah in Hebrew where it can be found in key passages in ancient scriptures. People then move the silence in an active meditation. I participated in several sessions of this co-creational light work and taught it myself, on five-day courses in Roslin, and shorter ones in Ireland. I have taught people from many different disciplines of spirituality and they all found the energies they encountered to be of the highest level available to them.

Several UK grids discovered by Lincolnshire-based geometer/geomancer Anthony Peart reference a strong connecting ley to Lindisfarne. Peart's specialty lay in divining beautiful patterns over areas he plotted with mathematical accuracy on regional OS maps. These patterns can be seen as the signature tune of an area, with the often intricate geometry summarizing the energy or quality of each area he drew. Often the places he focussed on had been inhabited in the past by the Knights Templar and indeed he calls his body of work "Templar Mechanics". He had never visited Ireland, and in the flat marshes of Lincolnshire he poured over the OS maps of the Burren and drew a signature pattern over a wide area encompassing the mountains of Ailwee and Elva. Peart allows for the possibility of higher dimensions in his life. He finds drawing earth grids connects him with those dimensions in an inspiring and even healing manner. When he kindly gave me the Burren earth grid he had intuited and drawn up in 2008 with the suggestion I created tours based on the grid, I was unaware of any grids in the area that belonged to Buehler's Reshel universal system of earth grids. However, as in many of his cases beforehand, I found that the grid dovetailed neatly with one that Buehler later pointed out to me. Before we examine any specific ley lines, that create specific earth grids, I want to stress the origins of this thinking. I see the earth grids as templates of consciousness for Gaia. I had a life-long affinity with the Burren, and in recent years had been drawn more and more into feeling that everything is connected to an invisible matrix that is slowly revealing itself to us. I was also more and more sensing the connection between vibrations and consciousness. I studied the system of sound vibration used in healing under Fabien Maman who understood this link well. He invented the term "vibratory healing" and seems to dwell in this invisible realm or matrix a lot of his time. I ached to understand what the Burren represented more. Since earth grids vibrate at subtle frequencies that are linked to consciousness, the grid given to me slowly provided the clues.

Beyond our own subjective interpretation of the Earth's qualities or vibrations, each sacred site has its own core energy with a universal note or tone to accompany it. It is a natural gift to be able to discern the core energy of a place. (I have been researching further recently about how all sacred places have key notes or sounds that reflect their essence, and which can be toned.) A story from my own life might help illustrate the gift of discernment:

About twenty years ago, I attended a conference in County Meath in Ireland, where I incidentally met someone who shared my interest in the sacredness of the land. One of the Dutch attendees was very interested in "reading" ancient monuments in the landscape. He found it hard to express his gifts as when he visited places of antiquity he was able to vividly see ancient ceremonies roll before his eyes. The sights would often overwhelm him emotionally, and then he could not articulate them, which in turn led him to feel a little isolated. He wanted to see Newgrange, as he had visited it earlier in the week but in too great a haste. He invited me to accompany him after the conference. When we got there I wandered here and there touching stones and sensing what their qualities were. He in the meantime wandered off on his own. Toward the end of our visit we reconvened and he asked me to describe what I had felt at certain places. I talked of stones being feminine or masculine in nature-and there were two large ones near the entrance with a third to one side which I found myself pronouncing to be the child born of the dark light. I did not know I was going to say such a thing until I opened my mouth. I saw my continental friend was grinning. What I had just said confirmed for him my ability to see beyond the superficial levels, to the deeper underlying core energy of the place. In addition, this psychic friend said that everything I went on to say about the site matched the visual ceremonials he saw with his third eye, and that my articulation of the qualities of the layout and stones made perfect sense in the light of the action he saw. It seemed to help him assimilate his own experience. This was the first time I had been told I had an ability to read the landscape or a sacred site. Others in his Dutch delegation had visited Newgrange earlier and had felt a fear at these stones, sensing an abyss beyond which it was dangerous to pass. If one can get beyond the point of duality and see darkness for what it is, an essential part of creation, one can realise that everything at base level is perfect purity and light emanating from the void. I view the pristine underlying reality to any site in the same vein that each of us has a core of beauty and purity – the same divine spark that Christ came to demonstrate lay in each of us. When we calibrate momentarily with that divine spark then all other layers fall away or are healed. The only way at a site to really discern all the layers or qualities is to first tune into its pure essence. From that deep core every other layer is seen as a valid and temporary layer.

Humans and other spirits have added the subtle layers to the pure essence at the base of any site. Sites that remain connected to their original purpose are protected though. Many people cannot sense this base and are distracted naturally by the overlaying energies with which they are more familiar. People can only sense what they are able to resonate with and not beyond. If you can sense the base line or essence of a place then it is more likely you can discern if the energy you are sensing is of your own projection or is emanating from the place itself. Moreover you won't get caught up so readily in the energetic drama of the place. You will receive automatic protection because at this level you, like the sites, are always protected. Anything emanating in your mind's eye is fully "Christic" or of the full light spectrum. You can also sense the frequencies and determine whether they are rare or common. The greater the range of energies you are comfortable with, the more you are capable of being exposed to high level frequencies of natural energies in the land.

Many years later I learnt that in co-creation, there have to be two opposing poles from which everything can begin. (This featured in the Lon myth where we have the magic cow and the magic blacksmith, or we have Fionn McCool and Lon "opposing" one another in a drama of conflict of interest.) In between these poles lies a central pole, which can connect with a monopolar, non-dualistic nothingness. In Lon's myth his third arm that protruded from his chest was akin to the third central, almost invisible leg/pole. The central pole connects to the underlying abyss, not to be feared but to be acknowledged and respected. Within that void, time and space do not exist. These are mental constructs that exist in our three dimensional world. Without that essential void or emptiness of space, nothing of import can be created. When I sensed a child being created from the abyss at Newgrange, it was because the site was still active with high frequency energies. (Sometimes sites are shut down after they have served their purpose, or they may temporarily shut down.)

Later in my life I returned in a more focussed manner to interpreting sites within a landscape, dowsing patterns of sacred geometry that all started with the still point in the landscape. The patterns correlated with specific coding the Knights Templar and later Masons used in their temples, cathedrals, estates, monuments and gravestones. I feel this knowledge is best approached with an innocent air of inquisitiveness, as there are no hard and fast rules on how to discover such hidden knowledge. I simply asked what all the patterns could mean, and then I came across William Buehler's work that enlightened me further.

After the layer of nothingness comes the notion of an underlying essential quality. Many grids in the landscape possess an essence that is paramount to understanding how they work. Buehler's grids reflect very complex thought patterns from the divine inner planes. Acupuncture points, such as generated at round towers, serve to boost grids, but are not necessarily anchors in the landscape. There has to be anchoring points for these grids so that they can work properly. The grids will anchor at certain points, only some of which are power points in the landscape. It is important not to imagine that the nodes of the geometry relate to energies that are fixed at particular points in the land. Such grids can do many things and are by no means static.

Sacred geometries facilitate growth and transform consciousness. When a grid is discovered in the landscape, it begs the question as to what subtle energies are represented by the pattern. Many early churches, forts and other centres of human activity fall on or near the grid lines. Certainly in the case of Anthony Peart's grid I have noted several human events that seem to reflect the subtle energies underlain by the local grid. I will relate some of these events shortly, but first I would like to look at the intricate and beautiful patterning of his grid.

Peart's grid contains two overlapping circles of equal size, one in the west and one in the east. Both circles contain three concentric further rings of descending size, the circumference of each in the westerly or left-hand circle matching the corresponding one in the easterly or right-hand circle. The two circles form their own mini grids that could be differentiated as an easterly and westerly grid. There is also a small central area where the circles overlap and form a vesica pisces shape, which was an early symbol for Christ. The westerly and easterly circles centre on the two great mountains in the Burren: Slieve Elva and Ailwee Mountain respectively. Under the latter lies

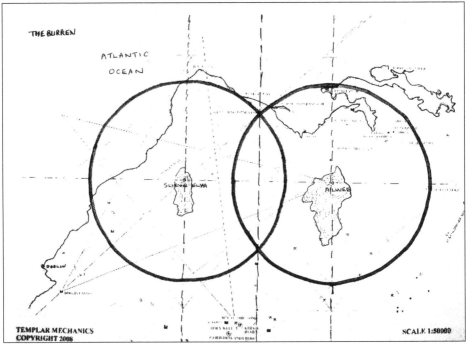

Diagram to show grid with two adjacent circles overlapping to form central Vesica Pisces, with three parallel "pillars" in dotted lines

the longest explored cave in Ireland. As a dry river cave it is a popular visitor attraction.

I did sense a lot of activity in the area where the two circles overlapped in the Burren grid. There are four lines intersecting here to form a cross in the approximate cardinal directions. The north-south line intersects many significant points in the landscape and is also the central line of three parallel lines or pillars - the ones either side go through the peaks of Slieve Elva (where I had my devic and essentially female experience in the hawthorn grove) and Ailwee to the west and east respectively Elva's graceful slopes of shale mask the underlying limestone that surfaces on the more jagged Ailwee. In turn Ailwee masks the deep cave system that has been opened to the public. We can view the pillars as female in the west, male in the east and the still point in the centre. At higher frequencies the polarities are likely to swap over and eventually a state of being is reached where no polarity exists, as represented by the central pillar which is, as mentioned above, monopolar. Monopolar energy systems exist in zones beyond our notion of time and space and feature in the Reshel developing system.

It is possible as a human to briefly experience these states of being. Only the spiritually adept can manage the energies of the central pillar, that are closed unless once can handle them. For those who can balance the male and female energies and evolve thus, the central pillar is activated. A degree of enlightenment ensues.

Nowadays it is more a question of matching one's vibrations than progressing through any hidden path of initiation. In the past the knowledge was confined to mystery schools and suchlike. For instance, the three lines/pillars were indicated an enlightened state of being that was echoed in initiatory rites such as those of Freemasonry. The central pillar reaches beyond polarities and its energies could only be accessed by those who had mastered the normal steps in their spiritual path. The knowledge of this is reflected in designs of Scottish tombstones of the seventeenth and eighteenth centuries. Usually in Masonic architecture this central pillar is less visible, as in the architecture of the Lady Chapel at Rosslyn Chapel where it is far less an ornamented pillar than those placed either side of it. At times when visiting the chapel I have overheard mystics call it the Ascension Pillar. Enlightenment is a prerequisite of the Ascension process. In the Jewish Kaballah tradition it is associated with transformation and the deeper levels of knowledge in the inner tradition. In Maia Nartoomid's work (10) I have seen her depict the pillar as a "Layoeesh Pillar" ("layoeesh is a word within a language of light she channels), with a spiralling of DNA particles wrapped round it to denote the fundamental changes that take place in the initiate. Interestingly just before reaching the centre of the Burren grid the central pillar/line traverses Corkscrew Hill. The endless hairpin bends reminded me of the spiral pattern Maia drew in her art work depicting the spiritual function of the pillar. With Peart's grid work we often found that sharp bends or tight corners and oddly placed gates were on significant sections.

When I first went exploring this grid I called by the Gregan Castle Hotel, as I mistakenly thought it was the centre of the grid. Perhaps the centre has shifted across the road from its mathematical centre, as in Gregan Castle Hotel there is a permanent rose garden in the shape of a Celtic cross - again matching the centre of the grid pattern here. In the centre of the rose garden is a gyroscope representing the world, with loving prayers in many languages inscribed on its base. One of them says "You were always held in the palm of his hand". I found this such a fitting motif to be placed near or at the centre of the grid, and learnt that it had been planted as a memorial garden for one of the three sons of the hotel owners at the time. Later when giving a talk on the Burren grid in the local village of Ballyvaughan one of the attendees rose to his feet animatedly when I flashed the picture of those beautiful orange roses of Gregan Castle Hotel. It was he in his capacity as hotel gardener who had been asked to design a fitting memorial garden for their son who had died tragically. He had felt inspired to create something special: a Celtic cross garden with a circular path round it. Now listening to me he felt a strong resonance with the grid. He too was very mindful of nature. Quite often it is a local guardian of the landscape that will unknowingly create an artefact that is in perfect alignment with the function of a grid.

On another visit to that magical area, having realised that the hotel was not indeed on the central ley of the grid, I arranged to pay a visit to the privately owned castle of Gregan, whose private grounds across the road on the hillside contained the ley. It was an old L shaped keep. Often such castles in Scotland are positioned on strong leys. Again this was significant as in the Reshel system the L is used as shorthand for a system that facilitates easier communications with higher energies. The Knight who makes an L move in chess symbolised a similar role in the game the Sufis introduced to the Knights Templar. It is known as the Eye of Ra in the Reshel. The long-term owners of Gregan Castle had been the O'Loughlins who had been the local chieftains for centuries. In fact, the Burren was then known as the Barony of Gragan! In 1644 due to the political upheaval wrought by Cromwellian forces the castle passed into the hands of the Martyn family, who were essentially descendants of the O'Loughlin clan! The influential Norman family of de Burgos (Burkes) had also owned the castle in early history.

Upon prior arrangement with the owners, I was able to successfully dowse the whole grid there. I learnt how the owner had planted many trees on his land. It is a pity that the brambles also grew, for I have never been so badly scratched in my life as I was that day tracing the ley through his woods! There was an ancient fort near the centre on one of the leys, and a very powerful dolmen in a collapsed state in the thick woodland. One tree bent its branch at a ninety degree angle to reflect the central line's energy. The pond below the castle was not directly on the ley line but nevertheless acted as a memory pool for all the events that may occur on the estate. I also saw a most interesting commissioned wooden sculpture in the woodland. Half human, half elemental, this extraordinary goddess rose from the ground in the central area of the grid. Her figure graces the poem at the start of chapter 4. Note especially how her feet are giant claws, which the owner later commented on was associated with a prehistoric "owl lady". Again, this symbol is most appropriate for the grid as the owl energy associated with the Reshel system comes from very high angelic realms.

Strong leys tend to inspire human action, and man-made signs sighted on the grid are often perfect descriptors of the qualities of the matrix. As I left the castle gates and turned downhill I passed another sign, on an estate gate beside the road leading down to Ballyvaughan. This gate was full of leaping dolphins that had been carved in metal. The dolphin is the creature associated with the global shift in consciousness taking place in our times: it is seen as the thirteenth sign in the Zodiac. 13 is an unstable or transient number that heralds in an upgrade of the traditional twelve signs of many systems, albeit at stellar, human or devic levels. Both the unicorn (with its spindle-shaped twisted horn) and the whale/dolphin (with its spindle-shaped body) represent the transition from one paradigm to another. Note the resemblance of the tusk of the narwhale with the horn of our mythical unicorn's horn. The transition always carries a lot of chaos, as that which is unable to adjust to higher frequencies needs to be discarded. Often this brings much human suffering in its wake. The much loved symbol of the unicorn has become more popular in recent years for a higher reason.

Likewise dolphin and whale watching have become popular pastimes. The area around Black Head nearby on the grid also offers opportunities to spot these truly noble creatures. Thus the dolphin gate was chosen to introduce the final chapter of this book.

A few years later, I was with two guests and we were visiting the old church and cemetery at Rathbourney. This is one of my favourite church sites in the Burren, as it has an old bullaun (large carved stone) lying among the gravestones, several old Celtic cross gravestones and a powerful grass-covered mound or chamber abutting the east wall of the chapel. The church lies on the east-west axis of the central cross of the Burren grid. Turning to leave the graveyard a gracious older couple stopped and started to talk with us. It turned out we were visiting on the anniversary of the death of the young man whose memorial rose garden lies in the grounds of Gregan Castle Hotel nearby! It reminded me how everything is connected always. The grids interact beyond the grave. I also learnt that the hoof marks of the legendary cow Glas Gavna mentioned in the Secondary Fire Chapter are featured close by. This is some way off but if you follow the ley line the hoof marks are on it leads to Slieve Elva, and from there you can follow the circumference that passes through its mountain peak round and it leads back to Glasgevnagh Hill. I think these grids impart a sense of how everything in time and space is connected by invisible threads.

When I first moved to Ireland I was living in a cottage directly on the southerly extension of the central ley without knowing it. Sometimes the clues are not so obvious and carry a sense of humour. The friendly postman Enda used to pop by for a cup of tea-one day I wanted to show him what I was reading since I thought he might enjoy it. He declared he had done enough reading to last all his life and doubted he would need to even look inside the cover. When I showed him the book he nearly fell off his chair - as it was the very title he had bought multiple copies of to give all his Russian friends when he was a long distance truck driver! He agreed the book "The Pillars of the Earth" by Ken Follet was an excellent book. It was only some years later I realised that the cottage was placed on one of the "pillars of the earth"! My immediate neighbour Paedar O'Loughlin was an excellent violin maker and a dowser too. He took me his ancestral village one day- and that too lay on the same ley. Meanwhile, the remaining neighbour in our small hamlet was talking to me one day when she asked me what the lines of light were she saw emanating from the cairns she and her father visited on a regular basis-again. Although she was not a dowser she was obviously sensitive to the leys. I had heard of Tibetan monks in exile seeing the leys as lines of light when they came to Scotland to locate where to build their monastery. Perhaps one day this young woman who rescues horses can put her skill to good use. It was Paedar who understood the qualities of his landscape in a deep fashion that is rare to behold and I am grateful to have been his neighbour for a brief period.

In the western half of the grid the outermost ring contains a hexagram that touches its ring at six points In the Reshel system, a hexagon connects with the divine heart energies and is the best form to make connections with all. I already wrote about this in terms of the six windows placed at regular intervals below the eaves of Kilmacduagh Round Tower. All the diagrams referring to the Burren grid are taken with permission from the

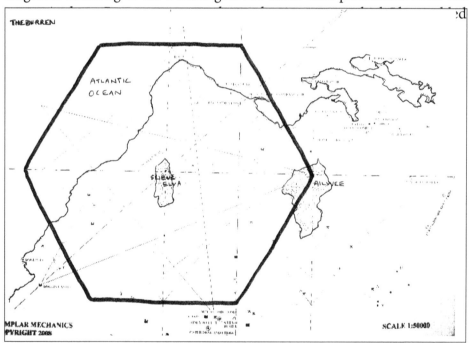

Diagram to show grid with hexagram in west

The east-west axis connects both mountains and in its western extension it skirts the northerly tip of Inisheer and the southernmost tip of Inismaan in the Aran Isles. There are also two upright rhombi (diamonds) inside each of the overlapping circles, whose apices touch their second and innermost rings - by rotating each rhombus ninety degrees on the spot, a lateral second rhombus is created. In the centre where the two circles of the grid overlap, a small third diamond or rhombus is naturally created. These diamonds can all be turned ninety degrees from their centre and then they touch the alternating circles. The two radii of the circles involved are set to the same ratio as that set between the earth and the moon! In other words the outer circumference of one circle is in direct ratio to the inner one in the proportion that the orbits of the Earth and Moon perform respectively. It is so appropriate that our own planet and that of the moon are represented in this pattern. The alternating diamond shapes are shown by dotted lines in th

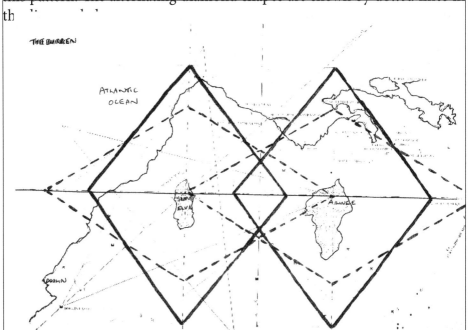

Diagram to show grid with east-west axis and rhombii

There also lies a large pentagram in the western half of the grid. Again referring to the Reshel system of interpretation, the pentagram is a seeding mechanism essential to bridge the non-visible with the visible manifesting realms. Meanwhile, the pentagram or five pointed star echoes the relationship between Earth and our nearest cousin Venus. The orbit of Venus takes approximately eight years to create a five pointed star round the Earth while she makes a retrograde progression in the sky.

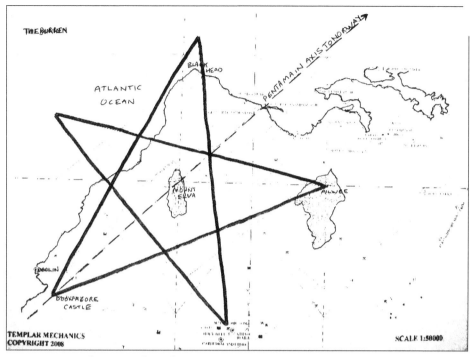

Diagram to show grid with pentagram originating in west but linking to eastern centre point

Most geometers understand that these two patterns represent the living (penta form) and non-living (hexa form) present in all life forms. We need the rational masculine 6 as much as we need the creative feminine 5 in order to have balance and harmony in the world. In the movement of the Earth herself, there is a resonant geometry created by the precessional cycle of 25920 years (created by the wobble factor at the pole) and the 21600 year cycle of obliquity (created by the axial tilt of 22.1-24.5 degrees) which presents a similar 6:5 ratio (7). The same geometrical patterning is present in human DNA, where the base compounds are arranged in hexagons and pentagons. We are, as Silva puts it so eloquently, a distillation of the universe down to our "biogemetric" cells. (11)

I would like to take a closer look at the western half of the whole grid that is typically more developed than the eastern half (in the Reshel grid system the eastern half is usually designated for the relatively unseen male seeding energy). The western half is overlain with this large, north-east oriented pentagram. The tip of its south west arm reaches the fairy-tale castle of Doonagore, overlooking Doolin. When Anthony Peart came to visit the Burren on a whistle-stop tour he noted with boyish delight how the tip of his pentagram reached Doonagore Castle, for its shape was the fairy-tale castle he had always loved. Now residing opposite the old Templar preceptor at Temple Bruer in Lincolnshire he often finds his earth grids bear testimony to the law of synchronicity. By drawing in the midrib of this arm of the pentagram, it forms a ley line that goes north-west through the crutch of two penta arms. The midrib goes through the peak of Slieve Elva and out to the coast at an unpronounceable place (written Illaungraffanavrankagh). The name is a combination of old Irish words that I believe stems from an earlier form of Celtic language usually spoken elsewhere within the Celtic kingdoms. The double "l" usage belongs to the P Celts of Cornwall and Brittany and old Britain (including southern Scotland and Wales). Could it be that there was an early Celtic Christian settlement here that left its mark in its place name? If these were Culdee monks sailing intuitively west along the leys that offered protection, there might have been an early pocket of Christianity here like there was in Scotland as reported by early travel writers. Certainly there might have been movement between the two countries before Columba and his Dal Riada tribe exported their Q Celtic language to Scotland. Even if the double "l" is an accident the vibration of the place may lead to its appropriate naming. One can walk towards the Rine a small piece of land that projects out to sea from the pinnacle well on a ley of the grid. Many ley lines cross the small road (boreen) and can be dowsed, and the sea wall of fine stone masonry admired. The fulacht fiadh (prehistoric cooking places, or arguably foot saunas) in the field, with the castle of Gleninagh in the majestic shadow of Black Head beyond it a sight to see, and its secluded well and church are very evocative of a time gone by.

On the same penta rib leyline there are some tidal rocks that feature in our story shortly. Eventually this line, when extended on Google Earth, reaches the town of Aldval at the foot of Trondfjell (means "throne" in old Norwegian tongue), a sacred mountain in eastern Norway that was a focal point for medieval pilgrimages. Like Lindisfarne, Trondfjell attracts leys from the UK and Ireland. At its foot lies Aldval, meaning "town of the Elves". Close to the other end in the Burren, the ley goes through Slieve Elva, and so the names at either end of the ley carry an interesting similarity. There is also a mythical sea voyage that relates in Irish how monks sailed to distant lands from the western shores of Ireland. In Chapter 3, I commented on these immrams being probable teaching aids for the monks in the early Middle Ages. The Voyage of Mealdun belongs to this category of legend, and while the lands described in the epic sea voyage seem to have no direct relation to known places, it is possible that the places described could have been inspired by real places encountered in early sea voyages. By remarkable coincidence, the aforementioned Norwegian writer Harald Boehlke lived for many years of his life on Trondfjell, where he had his own intimate experience once with the energy of this mountain. He had experienced a raw energy propel him to the very precipice from its height, an experience I had no wish to share! His research into early settlers in southern Norway highlighted the existence of many early Celtic crosses, akin to those found in Ireland, on the western seaboard of Norway! His research points towards Celtic monks from Ireland sailing to Norway in the late eleventh and early twelfth centuries because they held ideological viewpoints that the new abbots did not tolerate (12). During this time of Celtic influx there was a blossoming in the building of nearly all the main towns in Norway, together with their Christian cathedrals. Boehlke maintains the Irish monks brought their building skills to the disposal of the jarls for this purpose. In "The Norwegian Pentagram", Boehlke finally asserts that the new cities that sprung up at that time were sited, not by common-sense geographical factors, but by a hidden agenda that seeded a giant pentagram over the entire area of southern Norway to honour Norway's new affiliation with Christ! Since he was not a seasoned geometer at the time of writing this book, his excellent foray into landscape geometry ends with a big question; Why? His pentagram is very similar in shape to the one that hovers over the Burren, but in reverse orientation. His one points to Ireland!

Could it be that the final destination described in the Mealdun Saga was somewhere in Norway? Coincidences seem to point towards this. For instance, when I first moved to Ireland I stayed in a relative's holiday cottage. The very second I was leaving the cottage to move elsewhere the phone rang. It was a totally unexpected call from Eddie Stack, an Irish-speaking acquaintance who had just flown in from California where he has a home. I hurriedly explained that I was leaving for Spain for a month, and told him about the earth grid I was now in possession of. When I mentioned the ley from Doolin to Norway he became quite animated. Eddie has a keen interest in Irish literature (he teaches it in the US) and he told me that for him the Maeldun Saga had been about a sea voyage to Norway -

and he believed that the monks had set off from Doolin Point! It was quite hilarious that he had not heard of Harald's research and I had no idea what the Maeldun Saga was. How magical that someone whose expertise lay in Irish mythology should ring me out of the blue and alert me to a legend that seems to have a hidden message, connected to the earth grid I had been given!

The Burren Penta star faces the rising light of the midsummer sun and the associative ascending light. In the metaphysical Reshel body of knowledge I had studied, this north east direction is the best orientation for downloading spiritual light codes. A north east orientation connects with a mutable cross (cross changed to diagonal pattern) rather than a cardinal cross – energetically this in turn sets up the all-important eight directions that make the energies transfer between mundane and much deeper inner planes.

William Buehler had sensed that the Burren as a whole resonated at very rare chakra levels (beyond the crown level). He suggested that I played around with placing a basic Reshel pattern over the Burren grid, since the Burren grid indicated there was a lot of Reshel activity in the region. It often is the case that independent geometers discover sites that share identical nodes found on Reshel earth grids. In a nutshell, the Reshel grids act as umbrella grids for all other grids. At first I was unable to understand how the Reshel grids were capable of doing so. I later understood that the intent associated with an earth grid is the all-important factor. The core intent is crucial to the developing nature of the grid. Often geometers discover patterns or grids but do not know what they might mean. Buehler started off with the premise that he wished to find grids that supported the acceleration of consciousness currently taking place on Earth. His research led him to establish a dynamic meditation method he calls "synergy light work" which allowed him to access the highest realms accessible to humans. He then organised on a twice-weekly basis the quality of energies encountered in this sacred work. After years of understanding the geometry of the grids on a mental level I took the plunge and participated in the group process by visiting them in Colorado. This experience led me to subsequently conduct five day training sessions in Roslin Scotland.

It is difficult to find words for the indescribable beauty of the energies encountered in the sessions. The light work is a form of service performed at the soul level. Since all aspects of life are shifting rapidly into a higher vibration even aspects of the divine are shifting. We now live in an age when rigid structures are not required to create sacred energetic systems. I notice how relative newcomers to sacred work were capable of great work when accessing the high levels of divine intelligence without much priming. This is because of the purity of intent of the participants involved. They deploy a "heart-mind". We are evolving and developing new faculties to meet the incoming spiritual energies. In the end, the most complex things can only be accessed and embodied through pure simplicity. We communicate about various inner plane agencies involved in creating a grid as a means of creating a framework for the divine that is always ahead of us humans. However we are drawing slightly nearer the divine and I believe we are nearing the time when we can access the nature or consciousness of the Reshel grids at first hand, with intellectual knowledge only serving to further ground the grids. As an aside I feel that it best not get caught up in any fantastical future scenarios we read of from time to time, as that may distract us from the task at hand, which is to serve and grow according to our soul's highest purpose. If we trust in the Divine we will experience what we need at the right time by the law of magnetic attraction. It seems that my soul is interested in understanding the dynamics of earth processes. It is only one part of the vast uprising in consciousness.

When I came to Ireland I was asked to set up a local "light group" in Ennis. This "meditation group" was run on the same principle as the groups I used to lead in Roslin: we worked with the moving silence that is so essential in order to co-create with the inner plane's mentors to whom we dedicated the light work. In order to join the group there had to be some introduction to the metaphysical material, and my newest participant on a weekend training event in Ennis asked to go out on the land, rather than sit in and listen about sacred geometry. He quite rightly intuited that the land could teach him what he needed to know, and that he could embody the truth of material more by visiting the area where the earth grid lay. As we drove away from Doolin, one of the roads we were following for a few miles happened to be following a side of the arm in the pentagon. I was not looking at the map since I was driving, and he was not familiar with the area we were driving through. Suddenly I started to feel energies move and activate one chakra after another as we were driving along the ley line. It soon became evident that he was experiencing a similar energetic. We stopped the car and examined the OS map which had the grid drawn over it. We saw that at every geometric node in this grid we had both simultaneously felt a shift in our bodies. Often when I venture on the land, I am aware that the presence of a male consort will facilitate a deeper connection with the land. It is like we make a better whole when the complementary polarity is present.

I found as the years progressed that I could dowse ley lines crossing a road even when travelling in a car at a fair speed! When I began to dowse I always used to walk slowly round a site. I find map dowsing far quicker, although not so much fun. Chance encounters that verify the geometry can be very life-affirming experiences:

One of the first people I visited in the Burren ran a small enterprise from his home. I had been struck by his makeshift sign several times so decided one day to take the plunge and follow the signpost for "Soul Centre" down a seaward track. Richard O'Donohue greeted me with a benign grin, and soon I did not feel a stranger. First cousin to John O'Donohue, the famous (deceased) writer of best-selling Anam Cara and several other books, it turned out that Richard too practised meditation. At the time I did not have on me the map of the earth grid that had been given me to use, but I did, about two years later when I happened to be passing by and paid him another visit. Richard was building a curragh - an old-style fishing vessel still used by the Aran Islanders to this day. The reason Richard was building a curragh excited me. One day, while meditating, it was revealed to him to place a tall white pole on a particular spot in the Atlantic beside him. He then felt compelled to build a boat to sail out to the spot in order to erect this pole - the point in question was a short distance from the shore on tidal rocks called Farthing Rocks. I pulled out the map and showed him excitedly how this not only was on the midrib of the Burren grid discovered by Anthony Peart, but also it was on the Zayin point of another grid I had drawn up, using the basic Reshel "spear" of its larger pentagon grid!

Very often now Reshel grids are appearing that have no immediate landmarks to identify them with, since they can lie in natural wildernesses. It is common to find other geometers' grids carry Reshel patterns that lie hidden, as if just beyond the veil. It made sense for me to place the basic Reshel spear along the ley that goes to Norway, particularly since I had personal knowledge of both ends of the ley. Moreover Buehler stated that there were multiple options for overlaying a Reshel grid over such a complex grid, with many subsystems pointing to a very high vibration held within the land. The following diagram show the basic Reshel starting pattern, referring to nodes named after proto-Sinaitic letters Buehler researched as an independent researcher long ago at Washington University.

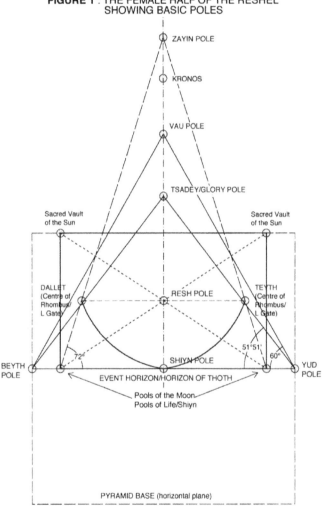

FIGURE 1 : THE FEMALE HALF OF THE RESHEL
SHOWING BASIC POLES

I was so content to know that while in an altered state of consciousness a local person had wisely intuited the specific Zayin point of a Reshel grid. His thought was like an executive thought, and in my mind it suggests he is a local guardian of the landscape. In most locales there are such people who care deeply for nature and the land.... The Zayin point is where the whole Reshel umbrella grid starts, being the most holy point at which to accept and sort out a vast array of spiritual information overseen by the Archangel Metatron. The Metatronic coding is then distributed into various patterns or grids. It is also important to note that no one ought to stand on Zayin point when designed within a temple grid such as Rosslyn Chapel. Instead there has to be a nearby point from which it is safe to access the Zayin pole or point. How fortuitous that the Farthing Rocks are tidal and so it is inadvisable to land on them. Further and quite poetically, the moon dictates the visibility of the rocks at night. The Burren itself has often been likened to a moonscape. A luminous white pole is a fitting symbol for the Zayin point-though to date it has not been created, which is okay too!

On another visit I paid Richard the curragh-maker he talked of a house in Ballyvaughan that had a lot of energy, which contained a spiral staircase (something my own father used specialize in making incidentally). I had intended that day to visit the Vau pole in the Reshel grid that lay on the landward side of Capanawalla a local hill. However I overstayed my visit and had no time that day. The Vau pole brings down spiritual light into the physical plane. It acts as a bridge between the envisioned and the accomplished, maintaining connections with all by using divine love energy. Later I consulted the map to locate the house Richard had spoken of. I saw it was placed in direct relation to the Vau pole using the curve of the the Vesica Pisces. The Vau pole lay equidistant from this curve as the house did on its mirror curve. Instead of visiting a natural site a human artefact that mirrored the dynamic it held with the Vesica Pisces had been drawn to our attention. This is just related here to show how conversations en route when tracing a grid can link in with the original intent and indicate another layer - often reflecting the state of being we are in. I view Peart's grids as more instantly accessible than the Reshel grids, which often have nothing of significance on the nodes of the geometry. However when there are artefacts on the Reshel grids they usually are immensely potent. The same is occurring with the siting of crop circles since at least 2008. (Crop circle designs have mirrored the Reshel for many years).

Once established, a Reshel grid will connect with many other Reshel grids world-wide, that continually upgrade the Reshel system. On the etheric level, they all work in synergy to support, create and assist in the evolution of consciousness for all sentient beings. Whilst the Reshel works at a high level, in reality any grids that are discovered all contribute at some level to the overall picture. It is the intent of the diviner/grid creator that is important when intuiting a grid.

I envision Anthony Peart's Burren grid acting like a bridge between the normal human condition and the higher Metatronic reality. (Archangel Metatron oversees the grids that are both galactic and earthly). That is why more events of a human nature can occur on Anthony Peart's grids than on the Reshel. According to Buehler, the Reshel grids demand that those who would interact with them possess a certain level of grace, or they shut down. In the past, only groups like an inner core of Knights Templar could use these grids to effect. Status and even genetic disposition was a pre-requisite to gaining access to the knowledge that the grids represented. Now individuals can access the grids provided their intent is aligned with them.

I noticed that some of the leys in the Burren grid followed St Colman's tracks. For instance, his hermitage at Kinalia lies below Eagle's Rock, on a ley line that is an extension of the northerly edge of a penta arm, whose tip is at Ailwee Mountain. (It is also near a fault line and the subtle energy of the geology probably lends itself to meditation.) The ley also connects with a holy well in the vicinity that is towards the nearest road. If you extend the southerly edge of the same penta arm through Ailwee Mountain you reach Oughtmama and St Colman's Well perched evocatively on the hillside. So St Colman was locating his sites along two sides of a pentagram. There are endless coincidences that can be read into these grids. However, unless it helps me realise what is going on, I can only go with it for brief spells.

Another ley extension worthy of note is that of the mid pentagram line to Norway. If this is extended south-west along the Atlantic seaboard, it skirts the entire Cliffs of Moher, where the sea waters meet the cliffs, and where the tourist boats trawl for good views. If you take that same arm of the pentagram and extend backwards on its northern side it travels through the much loved St Brigid's Well outside of Liscannor, close to the Cliffs of Moher. It also appears to go by the Rock Shop, a massive store selling crystals from around the world. It might be fortunate to buy a rock from this shop if it is on a major ley!

Outside of Ballyvaughan, on the coast road south, there is a holy well adorned with an ornamental shrine. This well lies directly on a ley line of the Burren grid. It can easily be dowsed and the same ley goes to Illaungraffanavrankagh on the coast nearby. This road affords excellent opportunities to dowse leys as the inner circle of the eastern half of the Burren grid crosses it more than once, as well as the mid rib of the pentagram. The whole area is very sweet in energies.

Holy wells are often placed on or near a line in the Burren earth grid. They would definitely boost the energy of the area as discussed in the chapter on water in this book. Humans consist of about seventy per cent water and so resonate well with it. I particularly like the placing of the holy well on the top of Slieve Elva. It comes as a complete surprise, as the whole approach to the summit takes you through the overlying shale of West Clare. However near the top, the limestone peeps through and water is able to percolate near the surface. This seems to be a pilgrimage station and offers stunning views of the Aran Islands. It would also be a place of "conductivity discontinuity" where magnetic levels fluctuate and human beings can feel affected. On the way I was drawn to a grove of hawthorn trees, growing in swampy land close to the track. Cotton grass danced in the wind all around and the trees were like two silent sentinels for the scene. I walked over and stood between the trees to see how it felt. Trees can create simple leys between them. I was astonished later to find when I looked at a picture I had taken of the trees that they were standing within a vortex of swirling energies that the camera had picked up on. Given that the ley goes through Sleive Elva to the Valley of the Elves at Aldval in Norway, I like to think of this as episodic fairy humour! Basically I regard Slieve Elva as more masculine and Slieve Ailwee as more feminine in nature, due to the nature of their underlying rocks.

The twinned mountain under which Ailwee Caves lie consists of limestone rather than shale. Gauging the centre of the Ailwee circles from my map-reading, I was sitting on the mountain when my mobile rang. (There is often no reception for mobile phones in the Burren so I had it still switched on.) The call was from a company in Plymouth, who have devised a process of implosion that they apply to water. They then place the water inside artefacts for purifying and energizing water, or inside jewellery for protecting the wearers. (The effects of such water implosions are similar to what naturally occurs in the Burren where water tumbles through underground streams.) Dolly rang to introduce herself and suggested I bought a piece of jewellery that was modelled on the Golden Mean spiral which is found in many life forms. Since I was seated on top of one of the grid's rhombic centres this alerted me to the Golden Ratio rhombus that is the second stage of a developing Reshel grid system. It indicated to me that Peart's grid was interacting with a higher Reshel grid. The time of the call was 15.15, which echoes the 5.15 mile radius that often features in Anthony Peart's grid work.

He calls it the Isis number for that is her gematria. I had often experienced number synchronicities when working with Anthony Peart in the past, so was not too surprised at the Isis coincidence. For me, it seemed to confirm that I had located the centre of the local grid section, as the grid attracts events to it. What better confirmation can there be than the Golden Mean spiral encased in copper and silver with imploded water inside?! I felt a quickening inside, as I reflected on how I was sitting on the Burren with its own hidden water streams. I wondered if any river streams were creating natural implosions below me!

Perhaps I have saved the best story up for last. When I first received the Burren grid, I set out to visit its centre one fine day in the early Spring of 2009. The weather was extremely bright and mild for tht time of year. So I decided to venture out and find the centre of the grid, where the east-west and north-south axis intersect. I parked the van and started to walk towards the centre. As I did so, I crossed a stream that was bubbling and vibrant. Blossoms overhung the brook and the scene was very pastoral. Filled with the joys of Spring I started to walk up a track I had seen from the map led to the centre of the grid. Rounding a corner I smelt something smouldering. I entered a field that was full of primroses and blue gentians peeping through the previous year's straw. I could see that many of the wild flowers were being scorched by spontaneous combustion that was taking place all over! I spent several minutes stamping out the fires and then contemplated what had happened. How extraordinary to encounter the element of fire when Irish weather is rarely hot enough in summer to cause this! I took it as a sign that this grid was hot! Acknowledging this I continued up the hill when on the final stretch while climbing a gate the mobile rang. It was a courtesy call from the Spirit Centre in Galway. I had never heard from this group before and how appropriate that such a name should ring me out of the blue! The woman tried to speak with me but got cut off. Once I reached the centre of the grid the woman rang again and started to go into such a panic that I suggested that we talk later. I felt she was picking up on the energy of the grid without realising, and it was too much to process. By being in the centre of the grid I was connecting with a powerful energy, especially as later my local friends told me that it was most unusual for fires to break out in the fields, and was especially unheard of in March. To discuss mundane arrangements with anyone while sitting in the centre of a massive earth grid is probably not a wise idea. I really felt that it came as a warning, to adjust slowly to the energies that surrounded me that day.

These energies reflect the Christic, or golden, essence that resides in all sentient beings. The colour vibration for the Burren is white gold. Linking with high chakras and new knowledge, wisdom and love combine here to bring us into deep harmony both within and without. Carrying an almost timeless quality, it reminds me of eternity.

1 The Divine Blueprint 2012 Freddy Silva Invisible Temple ISBN 13: 978-0-9852824-4-8 p192

2 Ancient Energies of the Earth David Cowan and Anne Silk ISBN 0 7225 3800 6 p24

3 Seeds of Knowledge Stone of Plenty 2005 John Burke and Kaj Halberg Council Oak Books ISBN 1-57178-184-6 p121

4 ibid p 10

5 The Spirit of Portland 2009 Gary Biltcliffe Roving Press p 5

6 ibid p 6

7 Ancient Mysteries Modern Visions The Magnetic Life of Agriculture Philip Callahan PhD 2001 Acres USA ISBN 0-911311 diagram and explanation p98

8 Seeds of Knowledge Stone of Plenty 2005 John Burke and Kaj Halberg Council Oak Books ISBN 1-57178-184-6 p173

9 The Divine Blueprint 2012 Freddy Silva Invisible Temple ISBN 13: 978-0-9852824-4-8 p211

10 http://www.spiritmythos.org/earth/ET/templamar/overview.html

11 The Divine Blueprint 2012 Freddy Silva Invisible Temple ISBN 13: 978-0-9852824-4-8 p208

12 The Viking Serpent by Harald S Boehkle Trafford Publishing 2007   ISBN 141209755– X 12.

SPIRIT OF METAL/ETHER (with relation to leys and earth grids)

Concluding remarks: The element of metal expresses itself in the mental sphere. When thoughts emanate from a divine source they can be expressed in forms beyond words, such as music, poetry and sacred geometry. In reality, sacred geometry represents states of being. In the earth grid over the Burren the frequency represented is beyond the normal parameters of our known electro-magnetic range. It is connected to galactic energies that we as humans cannot put into words. William Buehler, the world's foremost spiritual geometer, was able to discern this at a mere glance. The quality of the earth grid is hinted at in the final part that follows.

Element 6: Spirit of All Elements

Golden Promise
Cetaceous Promise
Leaping at the gateway
The harbingers of a new world
Make their out-of-the-blue appearances
They remind us to be vigilant
In order to be free

Chapter 8 Golden Child

The fusion of all previous elements gives rise to an additional quality that is difficult to define. I work on the principle that the sum of the parts is greater than the whole. After considering the five elements of wood, fire, earth, metal and water we see that a totally new energy emerges from the pentagram, which closely correlates with the central area of the grid. I see this is best described as the Golden Child archetype, which you can imagine placed at the centre of the pentagram. This energy is replicated in many sacred places on our dear planet. It will arise from the chaos of these times. This is our future. The chapter can only be called Spirit of Golden Child. It is based on higher love principles.

In the previous chapter, I introduced the notions of etheric earth grids which reflect spiritual qualities, or internal states of being, that emanate from the land over which they are placed. I made specific mention of a few earth grids that envelope the Burren - one of which serves as a universal umbrella "co-creational grid" for other more tangible grids to lock into. How do we accept and integrate these internal states of being? In the past, there has been sacred lore that can guide the initiate on their journey into the interior. Even today, we can reflect on this lore and use it as an aid to our own spiritual path whatever that may be. That is why I included some myths and legends in this book, for their meaning is seldom limited to their face value. Sacred lore stems from human consciousness interacting with the powers and presences in the landscape, atmosphere and stars (1), as we are creatures who look outward to our environment for inspiration.

All my life I have sought out places in the landscape for their benign influences. I was often unaware of stellar or cosmic influences, and yet upon reflection I can see that there have been many such influences that interwove with the landscape I was drawn to. My consciousness tends to find truths in synchronicities and parallel events, rather than in books or in gurus' teachings. Like many others perhaps, I have a dim awareness of spiritual guidance throughout my life. When I tune into sites where I perceive sacred connections, then I feel the spiritual juice flowing. It occurs whenever I travel. For instance, when I went to Dorset in the spring of 2013 to speak on the Burren earth grids, my host who met me at the airport passed through

Temple Coombe Village. I felt we had to stop there. Calling into the pub to sample the local cider, I found that the publican happened to be a Scottish Mason who had decorated his pub with fine old prints of Rosslyn Chapel, another sacred place with which I have strong connections. I felt I had met a guardian of the landscape, and that the southwest had officially opened its gateway for me there. When I returned from the trip, I received an enquiry for a tour from Japan (I lived there a year too) asking for all the major sites in Scotland I knew well, the Burren where I live in Ireland, and within England only one place; the Cerne Abbas giant which lay up the road from the village where I had been staying in Dorset. It is as if I carry the codes of the land with me, and others in turn are attracted to these places where my own consciousness temporarily resides. Places always leave a deep impression on me which I like to inwardly process.

When I moved from Roslin to Ireland, I was drawn to Gort for reasons I did not know at the time. I had no idea the area round Gort was geologically speaking part of the Burren, and indeed was older than the mountainous region I normally associate with the Burren. What was calling me?

Perhaps I can retrace some of the steps taken in this book to see what I can deduce. I looked at how in Ireland and Scotland the Culdee strain of beliefs lasted into the times when the closely related Knights Templar and Cistercian brotherhoods flowered. I had been familiar with that fact before coming to Ireland, due to my long sojourn in Scotland. In the Middle East, where these groups spent much of their founding period, they shared values and locations with the Essenes who had been driven underground long ago. (2) By the time the mediaeval groups spread their bases through Western Europe, their practical philosophy had grown quite sophisticated. Initial purity of intent is difficult to sustain on the earthly plane though - part of the human condition is to taint such endeavours. Eventually the vast and powerful Roman Church sought to quell the spread of the Knights Templar. In Midlothian in Scotland, an inner core of these knights remained for many years committed to the initial intent of the founding Templars, and Rosslyn Chapel testifies to a chain of knowledge that was carefully preserved. Truth never really disappears – it finds another outlet in due course. In this thread, it resurfaced in early Scottish Freemasonry there. Their spiritual purpose was to serve the wider community, by bringing heavenly energies into the earthly plane in order for all to evolve.

By comparison with the Scottish story, back in the twelfth century,

Ireland was becoming a most loyal subject of the Roman Church, and the Knights Templar did not last long - perhaps fifty years in Cork or Limerick according to one pleasant Mason I asked in the current lodge in Limerick. The Templars also were in St Nicholas' Cathedral in Galway, and Desi Kenny, co-owner of Ireland's longest standing bookstores, advised me that the Knights Templar probably used Ireland for refuelling on their sea voyages. They would have followed the prevailing sea currents round the west of Ireland. Certainly on the navigable Shannon in County Limerick, the unusually placed octagonal apse (chapter house?) abutting the north eastern side of the church at Askeaton suggests a previous Templar usage - and the Norman De Veres may have been their Norman benefactors at the time. Hard by Askeaton Church the Franciscans dwelt in a large, cloistered abbey, whose ruins are still impressively extensive today. I believe that the prevailing Culdee lineage took root in the early form of Cistercian lore, but that it too was quelled rapidly by the Roman Catholic Church. (I find Silva's study of the early Gnostic movements in Jerusalem reveals a close link between the Essenes and the later emerging Cistercians, and the lifestyle similarities between the Essenes and the Culdees are not accidental in my view). According to a research paper I read that was based on archives from the Vatican, the Cistercian order reformed after fifty years or so due to their practices being out of touch with the Roman belief system. Many abbots resigned at that time.

The remains of another Cistercian Abbey are set in a tranquil valley in the Burren. Corcomroe was known as St Mary's of the Fertile Rock. There are records of dissenting monks being expelled there in the twelfth century to make way for the Roman Catholic theology, as opposed to the Celtic one. While no monks exist there now, there is still a silence that inwardly moves many who visit, regardless of their religious orientation.

The Burren is a relatively large area brimming with tranquillity, beauty and magic on the fringes of Europe. It is not an area as well-known as Edinburgh or Rosslyn. However the principles of understanding the spiritual dynamics of the landscape remain the same. In the case of the Burren, I sense its role is more invisible and equally important to the future of human history. The Burren is a unique and sacred landscape that truly inspires a growing number of visitors and deserves all the close attention it receives. So what is this inner quality the Burren offers as a welcome respite from the twenty first century?

As described in the previous chapter, it is possible to place a Reshel grid over Peart's grid along an axis with which local actions have demonstrated a clear resonance. It appears that on the etheric plane the Burren conceals a significant umbrella earth grid. The overall pattern suggests that the land carries very high frequency vibrations, way beyond the normal electromagnetic range I spoke of earlier. They reach into the high angelic planes as well as the deep devic (elemental) or sacred earth planes. The energy the grid conveys can be summed up as the Christ consciousness. I refer to the Christ consciousness here as a divine state we can embody, rather than a historical figure. Christ consciousness is a perpetual process of becoming more wholly connected to source. This state of being is by no means confined to the domain of religions: it is a fearless state borne by unconditional, and therefore divine, love. For me the Burren grid reminds me of this possibility. The Burren embodies the Christ or Golden Child in essence.

We cannot underestimate the power of place to affect consciousness. Experiments recording electromagnetic impulses demonstrated higher measurements at powerful sacred sites than those taken at the same sites when meditation took place! (3) It appears that the spirit of place prefers silence to human chants or meditation. (I suspect that was because those in the experiment were meditating in an "entrained" mode, meaning that the sound was dictating everyone to vibrate at the same common denominator, rather than finding their own level within the whole. That would dampen down the energies to a commonly shared base level. Nonetheless, the experiment did prove that one can pick up energies quite effectively by simply being in sacred places.) On the other hand, the consciousness of Gaia seems inter-twined with our human thought processes. Our thoughts, attitudes and feelings all are part of human consciousness, which if focussed, as in the creation of earth grids for example, can make a real difference how the Earth feels! In general, our mental attitudes and state of being has to be considered in the current equation of Earth's stability. As one Burren farmer put it to me once:

"We cannot afford to view the land as if it were a mere commodity. Instead we have to view the land as a living entity."

For some people, the bareness of the Burren is frightening. In the Burren, the archetypal void is boosted by the underground river and cave systems, so the landscape imparts a strong sense of the universal void which is so essential for high energies to connect with. In many ways the void is the basis from which all energies spring. It is why on a subtle level, many people are drawn to visit the Burren. The landscape is undefiled and pristine. Its mysterious agenda moves you towards a state of pure being when you stay there. There are leakages in the etheric sheaths that surround the earth now that are allowing more spiritual light to envelop and pervade the earth. In an area such as the Burren where there is a high frequency earth grid operating it is natural to expect projects with new consciousness to take route there. This is because cosmic energies eventually affect human endeavours, impact on human affairs and bring about an evolution in consciousness. On the purest level, if we want to get more in touch with the Christ energy within and without, I believe the Burren remains a magnetically ripe environment for doing so. It is a unique and beautiful place to be on Earth.

So the Burren is infused with Christ consciousness. As a friend put it to me, she sees the grid as seeding a giant womb in the land. When the divine masculine grid infuses the divine feminine landscape here the energies co-create a union that is the Christ consciousness, or Christic energy, or Christ Child. Everything happens on a mental or etheric level with these grids. I understand that a grid requires a land mass to lock into and anchor itself on. Human recognition of the grid will then activate it. The Christic energy is generated by our witnessing the process.

I prefer to refer to this process as the incarnating of the Golden Child – a state of pure love that is the precursor for the Golden Age. As the grid evolves, so do we, for all is connected. Some are not comfortable with the image of the Christ child as a vital force. In light of more recent decades of new spiritual thinking, the symbol of the Golden Child has arisen as the new paradigm. The Golden Child is to me a motif for the Christ energy. I do not see the Christ energy as limited to any religious movement. From a healing and seer's perspective it is something that is happening due to cosmic forces that I touched on in the chapter on fairies (p 99).

Revealingly during the time of the Irish literary revival one mystical poet, George Russell, a regular visitor to Coole Park, Lady Gregory's home outside Gort, summed up the Christ energy in a personal vision he had. George Russell, alias AE, wrote of a vision of some child of destiny born when Ireland's future was to pivot round the fairy child of light born during the Winter Solstice. This describes an astronomical event occurring in our skies now. AE was a serious visionary; the child might not be a literal Christ-like figure, but rather an initiating stream of consciousness, borne by that void opening from within the vesica pisces formed by the aforementioned intersection of the Milky Way and the Zodiacal stars (4). Ireland does have a distinct role to play in the unfolding of spiritual dynamics. William Buehler put it once to me that Ireland can be seen as the innocent child or host who will manifest when the womb or chalice of the divine feminine is whole again.

On the human plane, we know that the Burren hosted a rich anchorite tradition which originated in ancient Egypt: the Culdees. Purification of thought was paramount to them in their contemplative tradition. What would their spiritual concerns have been? Whenever meditation and contemplation rule one's life, certain mystical facts become known. The golden rule known to all mystic paths is that form follows thought. The saints undoubtedly grew in self-knowledge, simultaneous with a sense of oneness with the Divine. This was hardly likely to be acceptable practice for a Roman Church which mainly sought to control, rather than lead its flock by humble example. The Culdee small prayer cells that doubled up as their humble dwelling illustrated the monks' quest for divine union. Their 13' by 21' oratories adhered to the Golden Mean proportion, which would enhance and harmonize their meditation practices. Their wells lay close to their cells, so they could practise outward ritual cleansing, both of themselves and of others. Aided by purification rites they elevated their consciousness beyond the three-dimensional plane of everyday consciousness, where they encountered creational powers on the inner planes (which equally encompass the devic/lower heavens and angelic/higher heavens). They felt the role of nature and the stars and the spirits. They observed their interplay. Like their Middle Eastern cousins the Essenes, who met on Mount Sion and elsewhere, they may well have witnessed the natural energies of Creation.

Jesus, as a historical figure, was of a highly respected Essene lineage, and in recent years many independent researchers have highlighted his background thus. In my view his three year mission taught people how to BE. From that state of being, all things flow naturally. Noting it is the message rather than the Messenger that is important here, Jesus Christ is said to have said

"The Kingdom of Heaven lies within you".

Our consciousness has shifted in several hundred years, as indeed everything always evolves on the inner planes. Nowadays many people toy with the notion of creating one's own destiny.

If the above message was taken to heart, perhaps many more people of all faiths or none would realise they have an innate ability, like him, to become God-like, basing their lives on unconditional love as the guiding principle. Perhaps Jesus Christ came not to create a religion but to show a way of living in truth and harmony. In Christianity Jesus, or more specifically Christ, has for many become a historical figure rather than a vehicle for expanding one's reality to a higher plane. This attainment of expanded consciousness requires a creative act of free flowing with the spirit. In reality, Christ's message was unimaginably energetic.

Clearly Jesus Christ was a most high initiate, who was able to draw on divine energies when working with the material world. By doing so he wrought miracles. He threatened the hierarchical structures of the authorities and the elders, whose work was based on false spiritual values and codes. It seems the Culdees preserved the inner knowledge for centuries, in isolated pockets on the western fringes of Europe. Perhaps the takeover of Culdee practices in the West of Britain and Ireland marked the demise of a spiritual kernel practice. The Culdees had taken special root in the Burren. Like those Culdees, we too can draw on the "Christ energy" to achieve so many things if we have the moral maturity and intent to embody these subtle divine energies. Such powers are inherent in the Burren landscape. Whenever we are only out to serve ourselves then those powers will withdraw.

When I studied theology, I sensed a passivity that saddened me to the core. Instead of empowering people to move from spirit and live their lives to the full in love and courage, everything tended towards over-conceptualisation and conformity. In the healing arts people have been awakening more to the energy they often call the Christ energy. This is a collective energy that embraces many subtle aspects of healing and creative energies. It does not have to be confined to those times when you visit a therapist though. We must reclaim our heritage to return to the right tracks. We are living in times to come when we can draw on the Christ energy within ourselves for healing, and much more.

We are far from gods, yet we are able to do far more than we realize. If we listen inwardly we might hear the quiet whisper of courage. I believe that we carry that same divine spark in us as Christ did, and that we have to wake up to our potential to co-create by embracing life's subtle energies and working with them for the good of all. By cultivating a strong inner state by whatever method or path we choose, we can persistently reach an innate state of grace. When we are akin to the state that Jesus proclaimed as the "kingdom of Heaven within you", we can start to create our destiny with a sense of divine inspiration. We possess a latent ability to become God-like, based on altruistic love as our guiding principle.

Until recently, such an attitude would not have been tolerated by ecclesiastical authorities. Church authorities were but one manifestation of the destructive hierarchies, all based on limiting spiritual values and codes that have ruled for a long time in society. Any free flowing of spirit within society would have threatened their position of power and control, and the comfortable status quo of worldly affairs they were intertwined with. The guiding principle by which human society can be transformed is one of love and equality, paying due respect to the natural world of which we are part. I imagine this sentiment is akin to that of the early Burren saints. Since we live in unprecedented times, when massive societal and personal changes are possible, I have hope.

The overlaying Reshel grids identified by modern day mystic William Buehler, work on a far higher energy level and cannot be measured with scientific instruments. William Buehler has identified the Sion/Zayin connection and role in earth grids that overlay the land. The Zayin pole is too sacred for humans to connect with directly in the Reshel geometry. How fitting that the pole is situated over tidal rocks that even sailors avoid! When all the grid is active this is the final pole to become active, allowing access into the higher realities within the wider universe. This is why the Burren grid is so important- for it effectively links to even greater universal energies than we are currently aware of! The ground plan of Rosslyn Chapel has a similar pattern of overlapping rhombi as the Burren grid has. The Zayin point manages both the divine goddess fertile energies in the more complex grid half and the male seeding grid in the other half. In the Burren grid, I view the goddess energy as residing in the west which is her spiritual home. The pentagram is mostly in this half and so are numerous forts and ecclesiastical centres. This book cover depicts a stone that stands at the gateway to the western half. She personifies the Spirit of Burren. She is the Divine Feminine guiding principle of Creation that the Reshel grid systems align with. The Burren has a Reshel grid, and it aptly contains a deeply feminine landscape. In the east, the limestone is more devoid of settlement, although there are a number of hermitages, and a well-known cave hollowed under Ailwee Mountain. This is the half where the male seed resides in esoteric tradition.

More remarkably, the Zayin pole is positioned at the tip of an arm of a large etheric pentagram in the classical basic template in Reshel geometry. The pentagram that Anthony Peart discovered has two tips close to the Zayin pole which lies on the midrib of the pentagram. These two tips lie on the outermost circle, as opposed to the Zayin pole that lies on the Earth cycle. If one placed another pentagram with its tips on the Zayin pole and so on round, there would be two interlocking pentagrams making a ten pole complex grid system, appearing like two interlocking cogs of pentagrams. This interplay makes for a highly charged grid. It is important to realise that the grids are only schematics for what is possible. Any higher beings are not attached to these grids – such beloved beings of light are always there, waiting for our souls to reach out to them. They interact with human souls rather than any artefact such as earth grids. The grids create an effect in which humans and divine intelligences can communicate if so they so wish.

For me, the Zayin pole, or node, was the most noticeable node in the entire Burren grid. Its onshore equivalent was almost the first place I visited. It is there that I met a modern day mystic, closely related to a well known and loved writer on spiritual matters (John O Donohue). The Zayin pole is significant in Buehler's Reshel system – and its name bears echoes of Sion/Mount Zion. Here, the Golden Child is incarnated through the Zayin pole – infusing all of Galway Bay, where the islands that housed Ireland's early anchorites lie. Due to the elaborate pattern Anthony Peart discovered, over which a Reshel grid extends its ley to Norway's pilgrim mountain, we can conclude that the Burren is a place in the physical, geographical world with enormous significance/potential for the evolution of higher consciousness.

I invite you to visit the Burren. May you be blessed by the white-golden rays it emanates!

1 Secrets of Fairy landscape Coleston Brown / Jessie Skillen 2012 Green Fire Publishing ISBN 978-0-9865912-2-8 p33
2 The Divine Blueprint 2012 Freddy Silva Invisible Temple ISBN 13: 978-0-9852824-4-8 P171

3 The Divine Blueprint 2012 Freddy Silva Invisible Temple ISBN 13: 978-0-9852824-4-8 p23

4 Secrets of Fairy landscape Coleston Brown / Jessie Skillen 2012 Green Fire Publishing ISBN 978-0-9865912-2-8 p82

SPIRIT OF ALL ELEMENTS

Concluding Remarks: The next part is your own story! I invite you to add your voice to the new metascience of spiritual geography.... What meditative landscapes have you encountered? What environments do you appreciate?

Postscript

This book was edited and designed by two separate people, both of whom did a large proportion of it while travelling on the East Coast Railway service from London to Edinburgh. According to William Buehler, railway tracks and trains denote ley lines when one dreams, and I have many dreams of this nature. I found this a fitting end process to this labour. For a book that talks of ley lines what better place to edit and design its layout than on a long distant train journey? It seems the gods are showing me some encouragement through synchronicity here.

For Further Reading:

PRAYING

The Miracle of Water: Masaru Emoto
ISBN 13: 9781451608052 / ISBN 10: 1451608055
By all accounts he is a humble man who has created beautiful water crystal patterns through various thought intents.

The Isiah Effect: Greg Braden
www.greggbraden.com
I read this book years ago and was affected by its implications on the nature of prayer.

The Neville Reader De Vorss Publications (2011)
ISBN: 9780875168111
This is is a collection of the deceased speaker's writings. I found it quite moving to read his beliefs and to glean his enormous powers of positivity.

John O'Donohue's books
www.johnodonohue.com
His book Anam Cara is a be a poignant reminder of the nature of the relationship I had with a deceased friend who called me thus, after having bought the book. I will always grateful for his friendship, which I still can sense beyond the grave.

DOWSING/ EARTH ENERGIES

Earth grids by Anthony Peart:
www.templarmechanics.com
The vault section is fun to explore for its beautiful geometries.

Ancient Energies of the Earth: David Cowan and Anne Silk
ISBN 0 7225 3800 6
A classic, written by a true gentleman. I knew David personally and we were kindred dowsers. (I never met Anne unfortunately.) I love this book for its simple accounts and scientific explanations of various earth energies

and phenomena.

Newgrange and the New Science: Kieran Comerford
www.kcomerford.com
A book written by an Irish electrical engineer, with a focus on Newgrange.
He presents a wide range of topics in his address of subtle energies.

SPIRITUAL ESOTERIC KNOWLEDGE SYSTEMS

Source channelling of Thoth by Maia Nartoomid:
e.g. http://spiritmythos.org/holyholies.html
A vast store of information contained within this website with artwork by
Maia too. Maia is a sweet divine person whose life has been dedicated to
the unfolding of deep cosmic mysteries. Her archives are second to none
and most "New Age" beliefs pale into insignificance when compared with
her breadth of viewpoint.

Archives of William Buehler:
www. http://www.shameer-orion.org/

Printed in the USA
CPSIA information can be obtained
at www.ICGtesting.com
LVHW010027120824
787986LV00010B/869